# THE EBOLA EPIDEMIC

## EPIDEMIC

## THE FIGHT, THE FUTURE

CONNIE GOLDSMITH

TWENTY-FIRST CENTURY BOOKS / MINNEAPOLIS

**Acknowledgment:** The author especially wishes to thank Karlyn Beer, PhD, Epidemic Intelligence Service officer, Centers for Disease Control and Prevention, Atlanta, for her valuable contributions to this book. This book is dedicated to the people of West Africa affected by Ebola and to all the health-care workers who risk their lives in the battle against it.

**Cover image:** A member of a Liberian Red Cross burial team in Monrovia in the fall of 2014

Text copyright © 2016 by Connie Goldsmith

Twenty-First Century Books
A division of Lerner Publishing Group, Inc.
241 First Avenue North
Minneapolis, MN 55401 USA

For reading levels and more information, look up this title at www.lernerbooks.com.

Main body text set in Apollo MT Std 11/16. Typeface provided by Monotype Typography.

**Library of Congress Cataloging-in-Publication Data**

Goldsmith, Connie, 1945-
    The ebola epidemic : the fight, the future / Connie Goldsmith.
      pages cm
    Audience: Age 12–18.
    Audience: Grade 7–8.
    Includes bibliographical references and index.
    ISBN 978-1-4677-9244-8 (lb : alk. paper) — ISBN 978-1-4677-9577-7 (eb pdf)
    1. Ebola virus disease—Juvenile literature.  2. Epidemics—Juvenile literature.  I. Title.
  RC140.5.G65 2016
    614.5'7—dc23                                                        2015025963

Manufactured in the United States of America
1 – BP – 12/31/15

# TABLE OF CONTENTS

# FOREWORD

As an Epidemic Intelligence Service officer (EISO) at the Centers for Disease Control and Prevention (CDC), I was asked to deploy to Liberia in September 2014 to help respond to the largest Ebola epidemic on record. I spent twenty-nine days in Liberia, a country struggling with the first Ebola epidemic in its history. Liberia is a small country located on the west coast of the African continent. The country is home to about four million people. It took nearly forty-eight hours and two red-eye flights through Paris, France; Casablanca, Morocco; and Freetown, Sierra Leone, to get to Liberia from CDC headquarters in Atlanta, Georgia. A week after arriving, I was sent alone to a county in Liberia called

Epidemic Intelligence Service officer Dr. Karlyn Beer *(left)* was in Liberia in the fall of 2014 to help respond to the Ebola crisis there. Her driver, George Momolu *(right),* is a US Embassy employee. He traveled with Karlyn for the month she was in Liberia. They brought and shared concentrated bleach with local residents and taught them how to mix it with water to make a hand-wash solution that kills Ebola viruses.

US Embassy driver George Momolu *(center)* helps unload a weighty cargo of rice and plantains from a truck that was stuck in a mudhole on the road to Monrovia from Maryland County. The truck caused a traffic jam that delayed Momolu, Beer, and other drivers, forcing them to sleep in their cars on the road overnight.

Maryland County, away from the capital city of Monrovia. The drive from Monrovia to Maryland County, a distance of about 500 miles (805 kilometers), took three full days in a car over rutted, muddy roads.

In Maryland County, I worked with local government officials to prevent more people from getting Ebola. In such a remote place that had never experienced this disease before, there was much to do. I trained health-care workers to safely wear protective suits. I helped to track and monitor people who were sick or might get sick. I spoke with community and religious leaders about ways they could help their communities to stay healthy.

My driver told me that before the Ebola outbreak, many people could be seen visiting bustling street markets. But on our drive, I saw mostly empty streets. Mud houses with thatched palm roofs were common sights. The houses were clustered together, often shared by several families. I noticed colorful plastic buckets with faucets in every village we passed through. The buckets were full of bleach water for handwashing. Before the Ebola outbreak, these buckets were nonexistent, but now they were everywhere I looked.

It was clear to me that Ebola had changed everyday life for Liberians. Hugs and handshakes, the traditional and common greetings in Liberia, were too risky because of Ebola. Soccer teams wouldn't meet for practice. Fresh fruits and vegetables weren't being brought into Liberia from neighboring countries. The efforts to confine the virus also confined so many aspects of everyday life.

I began a career in public health to help stop and prevent epidemics like this one. The people of Liberia, Guinea, and Sierra Leone have shouldered most of this tragedy and have worked the hardest to stop it. I felt honored to work side by side with Liberians during my deployment. Ebola is a disease with no geographic borders, and it can affect anyone. Working together, I am hopeful that our efforts to stop the epidemic will be successful.

*Karlyn Beer, MS, PhD, CDC EISO*

Microbiologist Dr. Peter Piot *(right foreground)* began studying the Ebola virus in 1976, before the disease even had a name. He was among the first to travel to what was then Zaire to learn more about who was getting sick, where, and why. He has gone on to become a world-renowned specialist in HIV/AIDS and Ebola. In this photo from 2014, Dr. Piot sits with Dr. Eugene Nzila *(left)* and clients at the medical center the two men founded in 1988 in Kinshasa, Democratic Republic of the Congo (formerly Zaire).

# CHAPTER ONE

# A RIVER IN ZAIRE

Central Africa was overwhelming. It was like flying over a green sea with a river in the middle. I was very impatient to get there and start working. When we arrived there and stopped, we saw three Flemish [Belgian] nuns and a priest. I introduced myself. "We're here to stop the epidemic and to help you." They said, "Don't come near. We're all going to die."

—Peter Piot, MD, PhD, 1976

**When the shiny blue thermos arrived** at Belgium's Institute of Tropical Medicine in Antwerp on September 29, 1976, it might have contained coffee for coworkers to share at break. Or it could have held enough lemonade for lunch with friends. Instead, one of the most dangerous viruses that science would ever identify lurked inside the thermos.

Dr. Jacques Courteille was a Belgian doctor who worked at a clinic in Kinshasa, Zaire (present-day Democratic Republic of the Congo). Dr. Courteille had sent the thermos to Antwerp. It traveled by commercial airline in a passenger's carry-on luggage. The thermos held two test tubes of blood from a sick nun who worked in Yambuku, Zaire, at a Catholic mission 682 miles (1,098 km) from Kinshasa. Mission staff suspected an outbreak of yellow fever in the region. Normally they would have returned the nun to Belgium for medical care, but she was far too ill to travel that far. Instead, mission staff sent her to Dr. Courteille's clinic in Kinshasa.

"It wasn't every day we received samples from as far away as equatorial Zaire," Dr. Peter Piot said. The twenty-seven-year-old doctor was a junior lab worker at the Institute of Tropical Medicine when he and his two colleagues received the thermos. "And it was clear this was an unusual sample, and that something pretty curious had occurred, because several Belgian nuns apparently died of the disease even though their [yellow fever] vaccinations were completely up to date."

The researchers wasted no time in opening the thermos. Not knowing the danger, Dr. Piot and his colleagues slipped on latex gloves. They wore no other protective gear, no face masks, no goggles. "We didn't even imagine the risk we were taking," Dr. Piot said. "Indeed, shipping those blood samples in a simple thermos, without any kind of precautions was an incredibly perilous act. . . . Unscrewing the thermos, we found a soup of half-melted ice. . . . One of the test tubes was intact, but there were pieces of a broken tube—its lethal content now mixed up with the ice water." The researchers fished out the unbroken test tube and went to work.

## IDENTIFYING THE STRANGER

Dr. Piot and his partners needed to discover whether or not the nun had yellow fever—a serious viral disease transmitted by the bite of infected mosquitoes. Viruses only grow in living tissue, so the researchers injected the nun's blood into young lab mice. They also injected tiny amounts of the blood into live cells grown from the kidneys of African green monkeys.

"All this work was done with no more precautions than if we had been handling a routine case of salmonella or tuberculosis," Dr. Piot said. "It never occurred to us that something far more rare and much more powerful might have just entered our lives." Eager to identify the virus, the men tested the mice and the monkey cells for yellow fever antibodies several times a day.

When viruses infect a human or animal, the immune system produces proteins called antibodies to fight off the infection. The antibodies are specific to the infective organism. If the nun had yellow fever, her blood would cause the monkey cells and the mice to produce yellow fever antibodies. But the tests for yellow fever antibodies were negative, as were tests for another tropical disease called Lassa fever. On the fifth day, the first mouse died. Three days later, all the mice were dead—a sure sign that the nun's blood contained a deadly organism.

The nun in Zaire had died the day after the thermos holding her blood sample reached Belgium. Dr. Courteille sent pieces of her liver to Dr. Piot in Belgium. Dr. Piot and his partners kept working on the samples, knowing they were not equipped to deal with the unknown virus. "Nevertheless, we continued to bustle around like amateurs in our cotton lab coats and latex gloves."

By this time, the virus had killed at least two hundred people at the mission in Yambuku. The World Health Organization (WHO)—an international organization that leads the world on global health issues—instructed Dr. Piot's lab director to ship all the samples of the virus to a high-security lab in England. Blood samples from the dead nun as well as the symptoms of people who had died of the unknown disease suggested to experts that a hemorrhagic virus had caused the deaths. These viruses can cause failure of body organs, high fever, and hemorrhage (heavy bleeding).

Days after they received the samples, the British lab forwarded them to the Centers for Disease Control (the present-day Centers for Disease Control and Prevention) in Atlanta, Georgia. The CDC was the world's expert in hemorrhagic viruses at the time.

Meanwhile, in spite of the order from the WHO, the Belgian researchers had not sent all the samples to England. They had kept a few at the institute and continued working on them. They prepared slides with very thin slices of mouse brain, liver, and kidney. Dr. Piot and his lab director took a look through the electron microscope. Dr. Piot remembered, "I peered over his shoulder and saw what were by virus standards, very large, long, wormlike structures, nothing like yellow fever."

The virus looked similar to Marburg, a rare and deadly disease that had been discovered nine years earlier. The workers in Belgium quickly bundled up the remaining samples and sent them to the CDC. They didn't want to study anything that might be related to the terrifying Marburg virus. The CDC soon confirmed that the new virus was indeed closely related to Marburg.

## THE HEART OF AFRICA

Dr. Piot and his team flew to Kinshasa two weeks later to join the US, French, and South African scientists who were converging on the country to study the new disease. "It was an overnight flight and I couldn't sleep. I was so excited about seeing Africa for the first time, about investigating this new virus, and about stopping the epidemic," Dr. Piot said. "It was my dream: I was going to the heart of Africa."

Government officials arranged a C-130 transport plane for the group, complete with a Land Rover, fuel, and all the food and medical equipment they would need. Dr. Piot greatly enjoyed the flight. "They [the pilots] let us move, one by one, into the cockpit, where we could take in the incredible vision of the tropical rain forest that flowed beneath us like a vast, heaving green sea punctuated now and then with a hamlet of fragile huts," he said.

The plane landed at a remote airfield in the tiny town of Bumba, near the Congo River. The pilots were so frightened by the mysterious disease in the region that they left the engines running while the team unloaded their gear. The pilots wanted to get away as soon as possible.

By then the new disease had killed many more people from the mission. Father Carlos, a colleague of the nuns and priests who had

In 1976 Sister Mariette walks among grave sites of colleagues and patients who died during the Ebola outbreak that fall. Doctors and nuns at the mission hospital in Yambuku, Zaire, treated the first known patient of Ebola. The virus moved quickly, killing at least two hundred people within the first month of its arrival.

died, greeted Dr. Piot's team in Bumba. He told them how the mission school's headmaster had fallen ill after he returned from a vacation in the north of Zaire. The headmaster had carried with him dead monkeys and antelopes when he returned, perhaps as food for the local people. The nuns had given the headmaster an injection of medication for what they believed to be malaria. He had died a few days later. People who attended his funeral soon became sick with high fevers, hallucinations, severe bleeding, and headaches. Many had died within eight days.

Yambuku was still another 75 miles (120 km) away from Bumba. Dr. Piot and his team lurched along rutted dirt roads in the Land Rover, past coffee and cocoa plantations, to the Catholic mission hidden in the lush rain forest near Yambuku. The beautiful red-roofed building, surrounded with immaculate lawns, palm trees, and a tidy courtyard, was a stark contrast to the fear that stalked its halls.

When the team reached the mission, a group of nuns warned the doctors not to come any closer. Dr. Piot approached them in spite of the warning. "There was a very emotional scene as the three nuns, Sisters Marcella, Genoveva, and Mariette, broke down, clinging to my arm, holding each other and crying helplessly as they all began talking at once. Watching their colleagues die one by one had been an appalling experience."

Dr. Piot toured villages for several days, talking to people who were sick, to their family members, and to the few people who had survived the virus. Doctors had to discover three things: (1) How did the epidemic start? (2) Where did the infected people come from? and (3) Who got sick?

Dr. Piot learned two facts. First, many people had become ill shortly after attending funerals. Second, many of the victims were young women who had visited the prenatal clinic at the mission shortly before

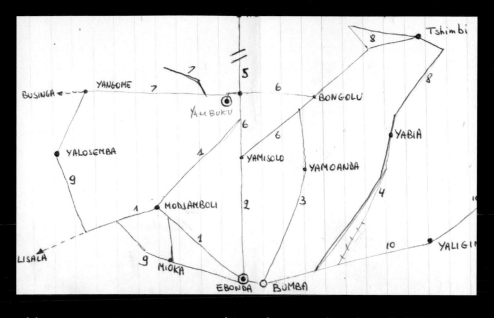

While in Zaire in 1976, Dr. Piot created a simple map to show the towns where people infected with Ebola were living, as part of contact tracing, a medical protocol to identify people who have come into contact with infected persons.

they became ill. The nuns typically gave the pregnant women injections of vitamins and calcium, a highly valued treatment in the local culture. The clinic had few medical supplies. A handful of glass syringes were sterilized every night but were used repeatedly during the day for injections without sterilizing them between each shot. It is likely that one of the syringes had been used to give the headmaster the injection of malaria medicine. It is also likely that the nuns then used the same syringe to inject the pregnant women.

"The nuns were totally committed women," Dr. Piot said. "They were brave. They faced an incredibly difficult environment and they dealt with it as best they could. . . . It was very hard to formulate the words that would inform the sisters that the virus had in all likelihood been amplified and spread by their own practices and lack of proper training." In this first identified outbreak of Ebola, the virus killed 280 people out of the 318 people it infected, for a mortality rate of 88 percent.

Weeks later back in Belgium, Dr. Piot and his team talked about what to call this frightening new virus. Yambuku virus, after the village where it was discovered? That would only stigmatize the village. This had happened before when other viruses had been named after towns. The Congo virus? Another virus had a similar name. In the end, they decided to call it the Ebola virus after a nearby river. "Actually there's no connection between the hemorrhagic fever and the Ebola River," Dr. Piot said. "Indeed, the Ebola River isn't even the closest river to

# GRATEFUL NATIONS REWARD DR. PIOT

Dr. Piot was lucky. He and his team did not develop Ebola despite their casual handling of the infected blood in 1976. Dr. Piot is also a pioneer in acquired immunodeficiency syndrome (AIDS) research. As a microbiologist trained at Belgium's University of Antwerp, Dr. Piot has worked with the United Nations and the World Health Organization and as a professor at prestigious universities around the world. He holds positions with organizations such as the National Academy of Sciences of the United States and the Royal College of Physicians in London, England, where he is based. He has written sixteen books and hundreds of scientific articles. News media interviewed Dr. Piot extensively during the 2014 Ebola epidemic.

The Zairian government appointed Dr. Piot an Officer of the Order of the Leopard of Zaire in 1976 for his work during the first Ebola outbreak. Senegal appointed him an Officer of the Order of the Lion of Senegal. King Albert II of Belgium knighted Dr. Piot a baron in 1995 for his work in an Ebola outbreak that year. He is also known as Baron Peter Piot.

the Yambuku mission. But in our entirely fatigued state, that's what we ended up calling the virus: Ebola."

Dr. Piot's life was never the same after Ebola. "It led me to do things I thought only happened in books. It gave me a mission in life to work on health in developing countries," he said. "It was not only the discovery of a virus but also of myself."

Under the microscope, the Ebola virus has a characteristic wormlike shape. Four of five identified Ebola species are known to cause illness in humans within two to twenty-one days of exposure to the virus. The four species that cause disease in humans are Ebola (formerly Zaire) virus, Sudan virus, Taï Forest virus, and Bundibugyo virus. The fifth, Reston virus, has caused disease in nonhuman primates.

# CHAPTER TWO

# THE EBOLA VIRUS

When we saw these worm-like structures under the electron microscope, we were all breathless and said, "What the hell is this?"

—Peter Piot, MD, PhD, 1976

**Not really alive, yet not quite dead,** viruses are the zombies of the microscopic world. They don't carry on any of the activities that define life. Viruses can't move or reproduce by themselves. They don't have any moving parts. Viruses don't need food or oxygen to live. In fact, they can't do much of anything until they get inside a living cell—a host.

Without a host, viruses survive in a kind of suspended animation for minutes, hours, or perhaps as long as a few days. Some float in the air inside water droplets. Others may survive in a small puddle of blood or water. If the right host—human or monkey, bats or birds—breathes in the contaminated air or if the puddled blood touches eyes or mouth, the virus enters the host's body and hijacks its cells. While some viruses are used in medical research, most don't seem to serve any useful purpose, unlike bacteria or fungi, some of which are necessary for life.

# OLDER THAN OLD

Viruses have been around for billions of years. Scientists believe the Ebola virus may be a relatively new virus that originated in insects millions of years ago. Virologists—scientists who study viruses—are not certain where viruses first came from, but they have three theories:

1.  *The regressive hypothesis* suggests that viruses originally began as small cells that infected larger cells. The small cells—or viruses—no longer needed to turn energy into food. They didn't need to reproduce. Why bother? The large cell they took over could perform those functions for the virus. Viruses then became inactive outside of living organisms.
2.  *The escape hypothesis* suggests that viruses arose from genetic materials (such as a bit of rogue ribonucleic acid—RNA) that escaped from a cell and gained the ability to move between cells and to replicate (reproduce) once inside a living organism.
3.  *The virus-first hypothesis* suggests that viruses came before cells or that cells and viruses evolved alongside each other.

Viruses cannot survive for long outside of a living cell. Most can only infect certain kinds of organisms. Some viruses infect plants. Others infect animals and people. Certain viruses can even infect bacteria. Where there is a life-form, there probably is a virus to infect it. Some viruses enter the human body through breaks in the skin or in the air we breathe. Others enter by way of mucous membranes of the mouth, nose, and genitals.

For example, the human immunodeficiency virus (HIV), which causes AIDS, is passed by body fluids exchanged during sexual contact or injected into the bloodstream, which can occur by reusing dirty needles. People get Hantavirus when they breathe in powdered particles of urine and feces from infected mice. Mosquitoes that carry West Nile virus transmit it when they bite people. The respiratory disease known as severe acute respiratory syndrome (SARS)—first identified in 2003—passes between people by viruses that linger in the air after an infected person coughs or sneezes. And the Ebola virus infects people who come into contact with the bodily fluids—blood, urine, saliva, feces, vomit, semen, and sweat—of an infected person.

## WHAT IS A ZOONOSIS?

Ebola is a zoonosis—an infectious disease passed from animals to humans. Many common diseases begin in the animal world. Humans can transmit some (but not all) zoonoses once they have been infected by the animal. Zoonotic diseases may be caused by bacteria and parasites as well as by viruses. People can get zoonotic diseases from contact with infected poultry, rodents, reptiles, amphibians, insects, and other domestic and wild animals. Scientists believe 60 percent of human diseases are zoonoses.

Here are some examples of common zoonoses:

| DISEASE | ORGANISM | CARRIER |
|---------|----------|---------|
| AIDS/HIV | Virus | Likely originated in monkeys |
| Chagas | Parasite | Carried by an insect commonly called the kissing bug |
| Ebola | Virus | Probably bats |
| Hantavirus | Virus | Rodents: dried droppings and urine |
| Lyme disease | Bacteria | Ticks |
| Malaria | Parasite | Mosquitoes |
| Plague | Bacteria | Mostly fleas carried by rodents |
| Rabies | Virus | Saliva of infected mammals |
| West Nile | Virus | Mosquitoes |

Viruses are between twenty and one hundred times smaller than bacteria. They can only be seen through electron microscopes, unlike bacteria, which can be seen with the common light microscope used in high school labs. Viruses are so small that millions of them could fit inside the period at the end of this sentence. Scientists measure viruses in nanometers (nm)—one billionth of a meter.

The Ebola virus, shaped like a tiny twisted snake, is about 80 nm in diameter and 974 to 1,063 nm in length. By comparison, a human hair is 80,000 to 100,000 nm wide. A chickenpox virus is 150 to 200 nm in size, while the measles virus is a bit smaller at 100 to 200 nm. Viruses come in shapes as different as fluffy cotton balls and bullet-shaped cylinders. One even looks like a prototype for a Mars rover. Under an electron microscope, some viruses appear as bristled spheres with so many spikes they resemble floating antiship mines.

## SOMETHING NEW

When Dr. Piot and his colleagues in Belgium first saw the Ebola virus in their electron microscope, they didn't realize they were looking at a virus that no one had ever seen before. The CDC in Atlanta soon confirmed the newly discovered virus was related to the Marburg virus. Marburg had first been identified in 1967 among German and Yugoslavian laboratory workers who became ill while working with infected monkey tissue. Researchers named it after Marburg, Germany, the city where it was first identified. The virus killed seven people and sickened thirty-one at three labs in Germany and Yugoslavia. Scientists placed the Marburg virus in a new family of viruses called Filoviridae. Ebola—identified in 1976—is only the second member of that small, but deadly, family of viruses.

The filoviruses—Ebola and Marburg—are among the viruses that cause viral hemorrhagic fever. Viral hemorrhagic fever is the name for a

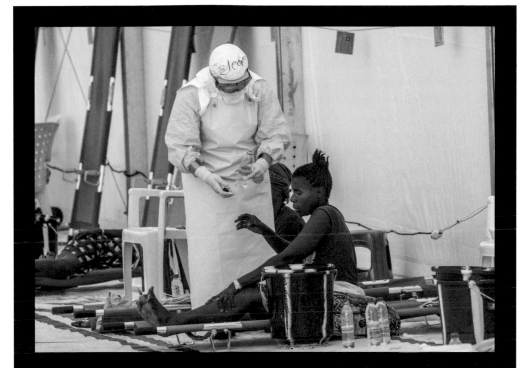

A health-care worker with Doctors Without Borders offers water to an Ebola patient in Monrovia, Liberia, in October 2014. The disease causes severe vomiting and diarrhea, which rapidly deplete the body of water and electrolytes. Rehydration is one of the first treatments an Ebola patient will receive.

cluster of symptoms rather than a specific disease. People who develop viral hemorrhagic fever become very ill with a high fever and severe damage to most body organs, especially the liver and kidneys. Viruses damage the blood vessels, and patients may lose large amounts of fluids from the leaky vessels. Patients may bleed profusely. Blood may appear in vomit and feces and may seep from the nose and mouth. The viruses that cause Lassa fever, yellow fever, and dengue fever can all lead to viral hemorrhagic fever.

Scientists have identified five kinds of Ebola virus: Ebola (formerly called Zaire virus), Sudan, Reston, Taï Forest, and Bundibugyo. Except for Reston, these Ebola viruses cause serious disease in humans and primates (gorillas and chimps). Reston is often fatal to monkeys but has little effect on people. It is named after Reston, Virginia, where the virus was first discovered in laboratory monkeys that reached the United States from the Philippines in 1989.

Structurally, Ebola is a simple virus tucked inside a fatty membrane made of glycoproteins—molecules formed of carbohydrates and proteins. The glycoproteins enable viruses to attach to living cells. These attachment proteins, similar to Velcro, allow Ebola viruses to dock with and then invade the host organism. The unusually long length of the Ebola virus gives it a greater surface area, compared to a round influenza virus, for example. This allows Ebola to attach more easily to cells.

The Ebola virus first binds to the outer membrane of a host cell using its glycoproteins. Inside the human body, Ebola viruses then attach to cells of the immune system called dendritic cells. Dendritic cells normally post a signal on their surface, like a movie star's name on a brightly lit theater marquee, to alert T lymphocytes (T cells) that the body is infected. T cells are the white blood cells that normally destroy viruses. If the dendritic cells cannot tell the T cells that a virus has entered the body, the T cells cannot attack the virus.

The host cell—usually a dendritic cell—surrounds the virus and pinches it off. Inside the host cell, a bubble-like structure called an endosome forms around the Ebola virus. Endosomes carry the Ebola stowaways deep into the cell, where they fuse with lysosomes, the waste disposal system of the cell. However, instead of being destroyed in the lysosome, the Ebola virus survives and is released into the cell where it takes over the cellular machinery. Soon newly made viruses bud from the surface of the host cell and move on to infect other cells.

As the new viruses leave the host cells, the cells die. The dying host cells release harmful chemicals that are especially damaging to the endothelium—the layer of cells that lines blood vessels. The destruction of the endothelium causes many of the worst symptoms that Ebola patients experience, such as shock and bleeding.

While doctors do not yet fully understand Ebola replication, it shares much in common with other RNA viruses. It is an inert (inactive) bundle of genetic material in search of a host. The sole purpose of a virus is to get inside a cell and turn it into a factory to produce new viruses. The virus enters the cell like a bully supervisor carrying its own genetic code on a blueprint. Once inside, it forces the host cell to provide the carpenters and electricians and bricklayers needed to build new viruses. Without workers to carry out its orders, the supervisor virus would be waiting outside, clutching the useless blueprint until it fell apart in its hands.

## SHAPE-SHIFTING VIRUSES

Viruses reproduce incredibly fast. It takes about twenty years, on average, for humans to produce each of their next generations—their children, grandchildren, and great-grandchildren. It takes bacteria half an hour to do the same. Viruses replicate even faster. Once viruses get inside a living cell and gain control of its reproductive machinery, some can churn out a new generation in minutes. Each of those newly replicated daughter viruses quickly moves on to infect other cells.

"Ebola's sucker punch is its speed of replication," said Ruth Tam, writing for the Public Broadcasting System. "At the time of death, a patient can have 1 billion copies of the virus in one cubic centimeter [0.06 cubic inches] of blood. HIV, also an RNA virus, has about the same number of viruses at the time of death. But unlike HIV, which only infects two types of immune cells, Ebola first infects white blood cells that disable the body's ability to destroy foreign substances, and then seizes nearly every cell type."

With such rapid replication comes a very high rate of mutation. Viruses mutate more in one day than humans have in tens of thousands of years. A mutation is a random and spontaneous change in an organism's genetic code. Some genetic mutations are harmless. Others are harmful to the virus. And some mutations favor the virus. For example, mutations may help viruses better adapt to their environment or make them more dangerous to humans.

It's not just the rapid replication of new viruses that's responsible for so many viral mutations. Viruses contain either deoxyribonucleic acid (DNA) or RNA, unlike higher life-forms, which contain both. For example, when a genetic mutation occurs in a human cell, the cell usually repairs itself so that new cells do not carry the mutation. It's like using spell-check on your computer to find and correct misspelled words before printing your report. But viruses such as Ebola are too small to hold anything as complex as a spell-check program. This means more mistakes are made, which leads to more mutations and the chance of increased virulence.

What might happen if the Ebola virus were to mutate? Would it become less dangerous to people? More dangerous? Doctors from the international medical charity Doctors Without Borders noticed in February 2015 that more patients were surviving Ebola. Patients arrived at treatment centers with fewer viruses in their blood, making recovery more likely. The fewer the viruses, the more probable it is that the human immune system can effectively fight back. Are patients seeking care earlier? Or has the virus mutated to become somewhat less deadly? A study published in 2015 found the Ebola virus was not mutating in a way that would make it easier to transmit or make it more deadly. This was good news. It means that the vaccines and treatments being tested are unlikely to be affected by mutations.

As dangerous as Ebola is, it is not an efficient virus. It requires contact with human body fluids for people to become ill. Ebola makes its victims so sick, so quickly that relatively few people survive long enough to infect other people. A group of scientists estimated the chance of catching Ebola in the United States during the height of the Ebola epidemic in 2014 was 1 in 13.1 million. Even in Liberia, a country hit hard by the epidemic, the risk of catching Ebola was 1 in 5,000.

By contrast, hepatitis B, one of the viruses that causes the liver disease hepatitis, is an example of an efficient virus. People with hepatitis B may feel well for years after being infected. They may not realize they are infected and can unknowingly pass hepatitis B to other people by sexual intercourse over the course of many years, leading to a high infection rate. It is possible that as Ebola passes through more human hosts over time, it may evolve to become less lethal and to kill less quickly, so that infected people may live longer and, as with hepatitis B, spread it to larger numbers of people. No one can predict how the Ebola virus may change.

So far, Ebola is only known to pass from one person or animal to another by contact with bodily fluids of an infected person or animal. In 2014, as Ebola spread through several countries in West Africa, the media raised the question: What if the Ebola virus becomes airborne like influenza viruses? It is much easier to become infected by an airborne virus than a blood-borne virus. While Ebola can be spread about 3 feet (0.9 meters) by droplets of mucus and saliva from the mouth, airborne viruses such as measles and influenza (flu) can travel 6 feet to 30 feet (1.8 to 9.1 m) in finely aerosolized particles that come from the lungs. Those viruses can float in the air for hours and infect people who walk through a room.

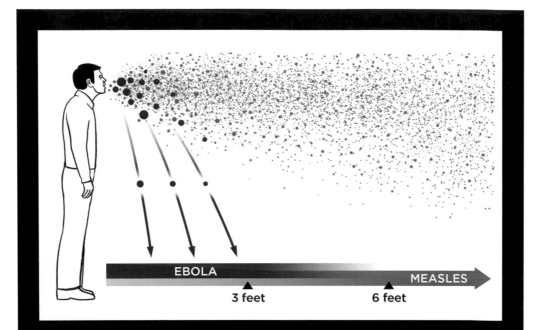

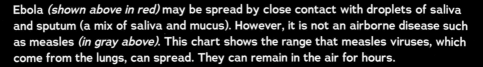

**EBOLA**      **MEASLES**

3 feet      6 feet

Ebola *(shown above in red)* may be spread by close contact with droplets of saliva and sputum (a mix of saliva and mucus). However, it is not an airborne disease such as measles *(in gray above)*. This chart shows the range that measles viruses, which come from the lungs, can spread. They can remain in the air for hours.

But many scientists don't think it is possible for Ebola to become airborne. A group of science writers said in *Time* magazine in 2014, "To be very clear: in the history of all viruses, scientists have yet to see a virus mutate so that it goes from spreading via droplets—meaning it is carried by infected bodily fluids—to become airborne." Why is this so unlikely? Ebola's Velcro-like surface has evolved to latch onto cells of the immune system that circulate in the blood. The virus would need to mutate so it has the ability to attach to cells in the upper respiratory tract—the nose and throat. Some scientists believe that particular mutation is unlikely to happen.

But the controversy has continued. In February 2015, a group of scientists writing for the American Society of Microbiologists theorized that it is likely Ebola may one day be spread by aerosolized particles from the respiratory tract. Another scientist doesn't agree with that theory. "There is no precedent for that happening in virology [the study of viruses]," said Dr. William Schaffner of Vanderbilt University in Tennessee.

A person with Ebola is most infectious in the hours right after death. Yet West African burial traditions include touching the corpse to cleanse and bid the person farewell. This explains why the disease spread so quickly during the first months. Since the initial outbreak, burial protocols that mandate protective gear when handling dead bodies *(above)* have been put into place, although not all families observe them.

# CHAPTER THREE

# FROM OUTBREAK TO EPIDEMIC

I am declaring the current outbreak of
the Ebola a public health emergency of
international concern. This is the largest, most
severe, most complex outbreak in the nearly
four decades history of this disease.

—Dr. Margaret Chan, director-general,
World Health Organization, 2014

**After the 1976 Ebola outbreak in Zaire**—known as
the Democratic Republic of the Congo since 1997—the virus
hopscotched around Africa. According to the CDC, Ebola
cases have occurred in Sudan, Gabon, Ivory Coast, Uganda,
and Congo. (The Congo is split into the Democratic Republic
of the Congo and Republic of the Congo). Ebola sickened
nearly 2,350 people between 1976 and 2013. The fatality
(death) rate varied from 36 percent to nearly 90 percent.

But these numbers pale in comparison to those of the
Ebola epidemic of 2014. Nearly all the cases of the 2014
epidemic were in Guinea, Liberia, and Sierra Leone in

West Africa. In just a few months, the death toll had exceeded that of every known Ebola outbreak combined. As of July 26, 2015, the WHO reported 27,748 cases of confirmed, probable, or suspected Ebola cases worldwide with 11,279 deaths. The WHO reported a death rate of nearly 41 percent among confirmed, probable, and suspected Ebola patients whose outcome was known in Liberia, Guinea, and Sierra Leone. That figure is believed to be unreliable, however, as outcomes among many other patients are unknown.

The actual number of cases and deaths was likely much higher. The CDC estimated that for every case of Ebola reported in public records, 1.5 cases were not reported. Some rural families didn't take their sick relatives to clinics. Instead, families kept patients at home and buried them in secret.

## FINDING PATIENT ZERO

Early in 2014, a large research team of US and African medical workers and scientists banded together to decode the genetic secrets of the Ebola virus. They collected blood samples from known and suspected Ebola patients in Sierra Leone. The blood held genetic material from the patients themselves, from bacteria, from Ebola—and from whatever else happened to be floating in the patients' blood at the time. The researchers sent the samples to laboratories at the Massachusetts Institute of Technology (MIT) outside of Boston, Massachusetts.

Researchers at MIT then decoded Ebola's complete genetic makeup. With that information, disease detectives began to search for patient zero—the first known case of a new outbreak. The search for patient zero went in a backward direction. By studying genetic mutations that occurred over time in Ebola viruses, scientists determined that twelve people had carried Ebola into Sierra Leone. Next, scientists discovered those twelve people had been infected after attending funerals in Guinea.

Going backward from the funerals, the scientists then traced the first known case of the 2014 Ebola epidemic to a two-year-old boy named Emile. The toddler lived in the tiny village of Meliandou, Guinea. Emile had died of fever and diarrhea, common symptoms of Ebola, on December 6, 2013. Next, his pregnant mother died. Then Emile's sister, three-year-old Philomena, sickened and died a few days later. The children's grandmother, who had cared for the sick children and their mother, died herself a few days later.

As friends and family prepared the bodies for burial and attended funerals, Ebola quickly spread from Guinea into Sierra Leone. Only a

# KNOW YOUR -DEMICS

As diseases make their way around the world, public health officials use different terms to describe how widespread they are. The terms often end in "demic," which comes from the Greek word for *people* and refers to how many people in an area are affected. The terms, in italics, are these:

- An *outbreak* occurs when a disease hits a few people in a localized region. This happened when the first identified cases of Ebola broke out in 1976 in a small village in Zaire.
- *Endemic* means that a disease is constantly present in the population. Malaria is endemic to several nations in Africa.
- An *epidemic* occurs when a disease strikes many people in several regions at the same time. Between December 2013 and on into 2015, Ebola sickened thousands of people in several African nations, making it an epidemic.
- A *pandemic* affects many people in many parts of the world at the same time. The world experienced two major pandemics in the twentieth century: the Spanish flu of 1918–1919 and HIV/AIDS, first identified in the early 1980s. The WHO labeled SARS, first identified in 2003, a global outbreak, but not a pandemic. Scientists don't believe Ebola could become a pandemic because it is not as contagious as many other diseases.

short boat ride across a river separates the two countries. Ebola then spread into Liberia. What started as a small outbreak in a remote jungle village became an epidemic throughout three countries.

## BANNING BAT SOUP

Scientists have suspected for more than a decade that bats may be the natural reservoir for the Ebola virus. A reservoir is the animal in which the infectious virus normally lives. For reasons that are not yet fully understood, the animal reservoir adapts to the virus and seldom becomes sick or dies from it. Over the years, researchers collected and studied thousands of bats in Africa and found evidence they had been infected by Ebola. However, the bats appeared healthy.

Researchers believe that Ebola passed to humans and other primates through infected fruit bats. Humans can contract the disease from physical contact with the bats while hunting or eating the animals or while playing with them.

Past outbreaks of Ebola were linked to humans hunting, handling, and eating bushmeat—wild animals such as bats and chimpanzees. In fact, scientists have long believed that HIV moved from animals to humans when people ate infected chimpanzees decades ago in Africa. In countries where food is in short supply, people catch and eat a variety of animals. They also may pick up dead animals in the forest and take them home for a meal.

For example, bats are a delicacy in parts of West Africa. People make a spicy soup from peppers and bat meat. Or they may grill bat meat over an open flame as some Americans would grill a burger. Cooking kills the Ebola virus, but bats can infect people during food preparation. In 2014 officials in Guinea banned bat soup and grilled bats. "We discovered the [reservoir] of the Ebola virus is the bat," Guinea's health minister, Remy Lamah, said. "We sent messages everywhere to announce the ban. People must even avoid consumption of rats and monkeys. They are very dangerous animals."

Ebola may also infect people or animals if they handle or eat fruit contaminated by bat saliva or droppings. Bats may pass the virus to gorillas and chimpanzees. In fact, a report published in January 2015 found that Ebola has killed one-third of the world's wild gorillas and chimpanzees since the 1990s. Ebola is more deadly to these animals than to people. It kills nearly every gorilla it infects and is lethal to three-fourths of the chimpanzees it infects.

But the 2014 Ebola epidemic started not with adult hunters. It started with Emile, the small child researchers identified as patient zero. Why Emile? Scientists announced in December 2014 that they were almost certain that Emile got Ebola by playing in a hollow kapok tree near his house. A large colony of free-tailed bats lived in the tree. Emile and other village children played with the small bats to see if they could catch them. This explains why a young child, rather than an adult hunter, was the first person in the village to get sick.

# CATCHING EBOLA

Not only do bats pass Ebola to people, humans pass it from person to person. Doctors suspect the virus can also be spread by contact with contaminated items such as bedding and clothing. However, the vast majority of people become ill through direct contact with the body fluids of an infected person, including blood, urine, saliva, feces, vomit, and sweat.

Ebola is also found in semen and may remain there for five months or more. This suggests that the virus can be transmitted sexually, so the CDC issued new guidelines in May 2015 advising Ebola survivors to use condoms during sexual activity until more information is known.

Once the Ebola viruses enter the human bloodstream, they attack and destroy much of the immune system. At first, patients may feel tired and have a slight fever. And without the natural defenses of the body's immune system, the viruses freely travel through the bloodstream to infect the lymph nodes, liver, and spleen. Injured organs release substances that damage the lining of blood vessels, causing them to leak fluids into the body. Liver damage leads to the release of chemicals that affect blood clotting. Patients may bleed from the rectum, mouth, and eyes, or they may vomit blood. Most often, however, patients die not from blood loss but from a severe drop in blood pressure that leads to shock and organ failure. Doctors believe people with Ebola are not contagious before they have symptoms.

# HAVING EBOLA

What is it like to have Ebola? Liberian ambulance driver Foday Gallah knows firsthand. He caught Ebola after taking a small child to the hospital. "I had headaches before, but the headaches of Ebola, they don't break." Ibuprofen, a common pain reliever, didn't help Gallah. "I have never experienced anything like I experienced with Ebola. Ebola

High fever is one of the earliest signs of Ebola. A medical worker takes the temperature of a woman entering Mali from Guinea to determine if she might be sick.

pain, it don't stop. It makes you want to give up. I used to be a strong man, and this just broke me down."

Liberian physician Dr. Philip Ireland nearly died from Ebola. He had severe vomiting and diarrhea the first two days. "By the morning of Day Three, I started to do some terrible, terrible hiccups [a symptom of advanced Ebola]. That was when the clinicians taking care of me thought I was going to die. They were discussing whether I would be cremated or buried."

In November 2014, the *New England Journal of Medicine* published an article describing the phases of an Ebola infection:

- Soon after the onset of symptoms, the patient may have a fever up to 104°F (40°C) along with body aches, fatigue, and a general feeling of illness. These could be the symptoms of many other diseases, including influenza and malaria.

- Between the third and tenth day, patients have stomach pain, nausea, vomiting, and diarrhea. Patients are highly infectious at this point. The fever continues, along with headache, chest and abdominal pain, bone pain, and confusion. Patients may lose between 5.3 and 8.5 quarts (5 and 8 liters) of fluid each day in their watery diarrhea. The loss of electrolytes such as sodium, chloride, and potassium in the diarrhea affects many bodily functions.

- The majority of patients who die from Ebola do so between the seventh and twelfth day when they enter the shock phase. Confusion increases. Heart and respiratory rates increase. Blood pressure falls. The kidneys slow down or stop working completely, and the liver is badly damaged. Large amounts of blood may appear in vomit and diarrhea.

- Nearly all patients who make it through the thirteenth day survive. By then the body's immune system revives enough to kick in and fight the infection. The bleeding slows and stops. Patients can eat and drink, and they have more energy. Doctors may discharge patients after three days without any symptoms and after negative Ebola blood tests.

According to the CDC, people who recover from Ebola carry antibodies that may protect them from getting the disease for at least ten years.

## SURVIVING EBOLA

In previous Ebola outbreaks, up to 90 percent of infected people died. In 2014 the death rate of confirmed cases was lower than in previous outbreaks. What changed? As the Ebola epidemic mushroomed across

West Africa, health-care workers became more knowledgeable about the disease and how to treat it. Patients who went to Ebola treatment centers had a better chance of surviving than those who stayed at home with family members.

Health-care resources are limited in West Africa, and caring for Ebola patients is resource-intensive. According to Doctors Without Borders, each day of treatment for an Ebola patient requires 53 gallons (201 liters) of water, 20 gallons (76 liters) of bleach, eight pairs of rubber gloves, and three bodysuits.

Doctors must triage (sort) patients into categories. Treatment depends on triage results and includes the following categories:

- *Patients who are dehydrated, but not in shock, and who can help take care of themselves.* These patients receive oral medications to slow diarrhea and to reduce vomiting. They drink fluids and electrolyte solutions to keep hydrated.

- *Patients who are dehydrated, not in shock, but are too sick to take care of themselves.* Doctors give these patients intravenous (IV) fluids to keep them hydrated. IV therapy is limited by the volume of patients, the shortage of health-care workers, and the scarcity of IV fluids.

- *Patients in shock and organ failure whose outcome would not improve with available medical care.* In nations with ample medical supplies, doctors can save many patients who have advanced Ebola. However, in West Africa, doctors must use their scarce resources for the patients who are most likely to survive. Patients already in shock with organ failure are likely to receive comfort measures only. They may receive medications to control fever and pain, and sedation to calm them as they die.

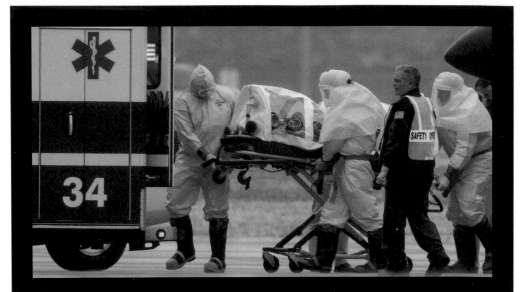

Dr. Martin Salia, a surgeon who contracted Ebola in his native Sierra Leone, arrives in the United States for treatment at the University of Nebraska Medical Center in Omaha in November 2014. He received intensive treatment, including kidney dialysis, sophisticated medications, a plasma transfusion from an Ebola survivor, and mechanical ventilation for his breathing. Salia was diagnosed on November 6, began treatment in Omaha on November 8, and died on November 17.

In wealthier nations, treatment is more sophisticated and may include oxygen and medications to stabilize blood pressure. Patients who develop a bacterial infection receive antibiotics. Patients can receive blood, be put on ventilators to help them breathe, and receive dialysis to replace the function of damaged kidneys. Plasma—the liquid part of blood—from Ebola survivors is filled with Ebola-fighting antibodies. Doctors can give this donated plasma to people who are very ill with Ebola in the hope of boosting their immune systems.

Advanced medical treatments like these are very expensive and are not available in poorer nations. For example, the University of Nebraska Medical Center (UNMC) treated two patients with Ebola in 2014. Chancellor Dr. Jeffrey Gold said, "At UNMC, it has cost around

$1.16 million to treat the two patients directed to us by the federal government. Treatment costs vary based on the severity of the patient when they arrive, but the cost is well beyond the normal costs incurred for an intensive care patient." He urged the federal government to reimburse US hospitals that have treated Ebola patients, because some of the costs—such as those for experimental treatments—are not covered by private health insurance.

## CONTACT TRACING

There's more to an epidemic than the people who are sick. Humans are social creatures with frequent contact with other people. Contact tracing is an important part of keeping a disease from spreading. Health-care workers or community volunteers talk to Ebola patients and their families. They identify and locate other people who came in close contact with the patient. This could be extended family, friends, or even strangers in the local market. Those people may have been exposed to Ebola and could spread it to others.

Once community workers identify all of an Ebola patient's contacts, health-care staff must decide who is at risk for developing Ebola. They question the contacts about Ebola symptoms to determine if they've been infected or not. All contacts should be monitored for fever and other symptoms of Ebola for twenty-one days. Anyone with symptoms should be admitted to an Ebola clinic for care.

The CDC classifies contacts as the following:

- *Low risk:* having been in a country with widespread Ebola cases within the past twenty-one days, shaking hands with a person in the early stage of Ebola, being in the same room for a brief time with a sick Ebola patient, or traveling on an airplane with someone with Ebola who had symptoms

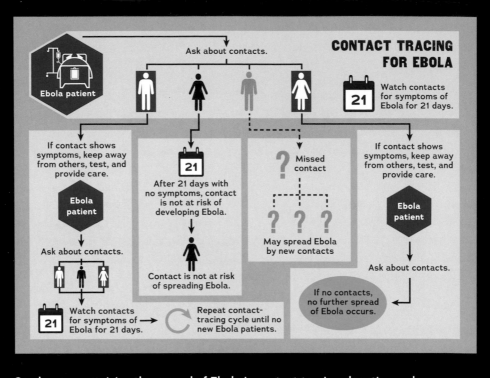

**CONTACT TRACING FOR EBOLA**

Ask about contacts.

Ebola patient

Watch contacts for symptoms of Ebola for 21 days.

If contact shows symptoms, keep away from others, test, and provide care.

Ebola patient

Ask about contacts.

Watch contacts for symptoms of Ebola for 21 days.

Repeat contact-tracing cycle until no new Ebola patients.

After 21 days with no symptoms, contact is not at risk of developing Ebola.

Contact is not at risk of spreading Ebola.

Missed contact

May spread Ebola by new contacts

If contact shows symptoms, keep away from others, test, and provide care.

Ebola patient

Ask about contacts.

If no contacts, no further spread of Ebola occurs.

**One key to containing the spread of Ebola is contact tracing—locating and interviewing the close contacts of people with the disease.**

- *Some risk:* direct contact with an Ebola patient or with body fluids while wearing appropriate protective gear, or being close for a prolonged period of time without protective gear to someone who had Ebola, such as happens in a family or household

- *High risk:* direct contact (without wearing protective gear) with body fluids of a person with Ebola who is having symptoms, processing blood of a sick Ebola patient without protective gear or biosafety precautions found in a laboratory, having lived in the immediate household and provided direct care to an Ebola patient, or direct contact with a dead body without protective gear

Health-care workers and public health officials take action to monitor or restrict movement of contacts based on their risk levels. Monitoring includes the following:

- *Active monitoring.* People who have been—or might have been—exposed to Ebola may be actively monitored in their home. Health officials visit at least once daily to check for fever or development of symptoms. A second check may occur in person or by phone.
- *Controlled movement.* Health officials may limit the movement of some people. For example, a person at risk for Ebola may not be allowed to travel by public transportation. Travel may be allowed by private vehicle if ongoing monitoring is arranged.
- *Quarantine and isolation.* People exposed to a contagious disease such as Ebola can be quarantined by public health officials. People in quarantine must be separated from people who have not been exposed. Often people in quarantine who are well may remain at home. The quarantine is lifted after twenty-one days if the person does not get sick. People who have symptoms are isolated from people who are not sick. Quarantine and isolation help to prevent spread of the disease.

The US government has the legal authority to quarantine and isolate people. The government assigns that role to the CDC. Quarantine and isolation are authorized for several diseases such as certain cases of drug-resistant tuberculosis, SARS, pandemic influenza, and viral hemorrhagic fevers—which include Ebola.

Fencing around Ebola treatment units in West Africa allowed for careful control of entrance into and exiting from the facilities. A staff member of a Doctors Without Borders facility takes a break at a gate in one of the Liberian units.

# CHAPTER FOUR

# PROTECTING THE PROTECTORS

We should be honoring, not quarantining, health-care workers who put their lives at risk not only to save people suffering from Ebola virus disease in West Africa but also to help achieve source control, bringing the world closer to stopping the spread of this killer epidemic.

—*New England Journal of Medicine*, editorial, 2014

**The death rate of the 2014** Ebola epidemic was even worse for health-care workers than it was for patients. As of July 26, 2015, the WHO had identified 880 confirmed cases of Ebola among health-care workers, more than 510 of whom had died, for a fatality rate of 58 percent. Shortages of protective gear and lack of training in how to use it contributed to the high infection rate among health-care workers when Ebola first emerged, according to the WHO. Health-care workers often worked long hours under very difficult conditions. Fatigue and stress can lead to errors that increase the possibility of infection.

*Left:* Infectious disease specialist Dr. Florian Steiner *(right)* and quarantine office leader Dr. Thomas Klotzkowski disinfect themselves during a demonstration of decontamination and doffing protocol at a hospital in Berlin, Germany. *Right:* In West Africa, a Liberian Red Cross worker disinfects a colleague in Banjol, Liberia, but without the benefit of an isolation ward. Health-care workers are most at risk of becoming infected because they typically work with patients at their sickest or when they are dying, when the virus is at its most contagious.

Dr. Peter Piot noted, "The mortality to medical staff and nurses has been enormous and devastating. Our colleagues are the most affected of all professions, paying a high price for their work."

During the early months of the epidemic, far too few health-care workers were available to take care of the large number of Ebola patients in West Africa. The region's health systems have very little money compared to those of the United States. Before the epidemic, West Africa had 1 doctor for every 71,000 people, while the United States had 1 doctor for every 400 people. The shortage of nurses was especially devastating. The United States had nearly 100 nurses for every 10,000 patients. Sierra Leone had 2 nurses for every 10,000 patients, while Liberia had 3. An additional 5,000 health-care workers were needed in the area to deal with the emerging crisis.

Dr. Rick Sacra, a US missionary who contracted Ebola in Liberia in 2014, recalled his treatment before the US State Department evacuated him to a US hospital. He noted that each nurse cared for fifteen to twenty seriously ill patients. "A nurse makes rounds maybe once every eight hours," Dr. Sacra said. "A doctor came by once a day. The staff is so few." Nurses in US intensive care units typically have one or two patients to care for, and they monitor their patients hour by hour. Dr. Sacra recovered completely, and in January 2015, he returned to Liberia to work with Ebola patients once more. Experts believe he is now immune to Ebola. "I don't plan to test that," he said. "I don't plan to forego protective gear or play with live bats while I'm there."

# Personal Protection

Searing heat. Steaming humidity. Long hours. High stress. Too few doctors and nurses. The continual possibility of accidental infection and death. A health-care system in shambles. In spite of these conditions, health-care workers from around the world volunteered to care for Ebola patients in West Africa. Even so, there were far too few.

At the height of the crisis in 2014, US and Liberian health officials developed a plan to encourage more doctors and nurses to work in Ebola-stricken regions. To reassure workers about the safety of working in West Africa, the US Department of Defense built a modern-day mobile army surgical hospital (MASH) unit—now called modular trauma hospitals—in Monrovia, Liberia, to treat any infected health-care workers from Liberia, the United States, and other countries. The Monrovia Medical Unit, as it was called, was designed to ensure that medical workers who became infected would receive high-quality medical care.

Members of the US Public Health Service staffed the twenty-five bed hospital built near Liberia's capital, Monrovia. Jamal Gwathney, a US doctor with the team at the new hospital, said, "All of us here are trying to convey to the world that you can come here as a health-care worker and provide care that's greatly needed, and if something were to happen to you, we'll give you the best care."

As promising as the Monrovia Medical Unit was, the first line of defense against Ebola for health-care workers is protective clothing. Personal protective equipment (PPE) seals people from head to foot in waterproof suits, aprons, face masks, goggles, boots, and a double set of gloves. In advanced medical centers such as those in the United States, the PPE may contain a portable air exchange system to prevent overheating.

The CDC developed detailed protocols for the use of PPE in US hospitals. The protocol for donning (putting on) PPE calls for twelve to fourteen steps. The greatest danger for becoming infected comes with doffing (taking off) PPE. After working with Ebola patients, PPE is heavily contaminated with infected bodily fluids.

Sanitized protective gear worn to bury or cremate Ebola victims dries outdoors at a Ministry of Health treatment center in Monrovia, Liberia. Doctors and health-care workers caring for Ebola patients must also wear clothing, boots, and gloves to protect themselves from the exposure to the virus.

CDC protocol lists up to twenty-four steps for doffing. Doffing may take about forty-five minutes and must be completed under the careful eye of an observer. Some experts believe the main mode of transmission of Ebola is not through a break in the skin but through mucous membranes of the eyes, nose, and mouth. Tiny droplets of infected fluids can fly off PPE and into the face during doffing, if not done correctly.

Procedures developed in the United States may not work in rural clinics in West Africa, however. Resources, space, and training are limited. Health-care workers are few, while patients are many. The climate is brutally hot and humid. Health-care workers dressed in PPE may lose 1 quart (0.9 liters) of sweat an hour. They may be limited to one or two hours of patient care at a time because they overheat so quickly wearing PPE. Portable air exchange units were generally unavailable in West Africa.

Dr. Colin Bucks, who also worked in a Liberian Ebola clinic, said, "You're soaked with sweat before you walk [into the patient rooms]. You're just drenched. The tough part is that when the masks get filled with your own breath and sweat, then it really gets hard to breathe. . . . You have to get out then. It actually feels like you're suffocating."

Pares Momanyi, a nursing supervisor in an Ebola treatment center in Liberia said, "When I go in, we chat with [the patients], ask how they're doing, how they are feeling, whether they are in pain. They need love. They need reassurance. . . . You can talk softly, rub their back, hold their hand. You want to take off the mask so that they see that you're feeling what they're going through. But you can't." But no matter the difficulties with its use, PPE can be the difference between life and death for health-care workers.

Another important part of protecting health-care workers is the proper use of chlorine (such as found in household bleach) disinfecting solution for handwashing. Dr. Karlyn Beer, Epidemic Intelligence

US Embassy driver George Momolu washes his hands in a roadside bucket of chlorinated water at a military checkpoint in Nimba County, Liberia. This simple protocol for killing the Ebola virus was implemented throughout West Africa in all public settings and in private homes.

Service officer with the CDC, worked in Liberia on the Ebola response in 2014. "Two housekeepers asked me why chlorine was important for hand washing and how to make the diluted chlorine water," she says. "I explained that chlorine kills the virus and showed them how to measure out a 0.05% chlorine solution using a spoon and a typical bucket found in Liberian homes. Even though English is an official language in Liberia, I drew pictures of buckets and spoons to illustrate my instructions so they could make the correct solution. No matter where a person is from, pictures are often an easier way to learn compared with spoken instructions."

# CLINICS THAT CARE

Ebola clinics in West Africa may look a little different depending on who built them, but they share several elements. The clinic grounds are typically divided into three sections: one for low-risk patients, one for high-risk suspected cases, and another for confirmed cases.

Doctors Without Borders was the first organizations to respond to the Ebola epidemic. The group built a large Ebola treatment center in Paynesville, Liberia (and other sites as well). The clinic demonstrates the features of an ideal Ebola clinic, including areas where patients can talk with their family from a safe distance.

Staff enters through one gate into the low-risk area that includes meeting rooms, showers, supplies, and offices. Health-care workers who will care for Ebola patients that day move directly to the changing area. After donning PPE, staff exits the low-risk area and enters the high-risk suspected area. They visit patients who are suspected of having Ebola to see how they're doing, and they check if test results have come back. While patients wait to find out if they have Ebola or not, they are housed in nonmedical wards and have their own bathroom facilities.

Patients who are known to have Ebola enter the third zone—the high-risk confirmed cases zone. Staff cares for confirmed patients in the treatment wards. Some patients can walk and take care of themselves, so bathroom facilities and showers are available for their use.

Patients who test negative for Ebola leave the high-risk zone through an exit for cured patients. At the end of their shifts, health-care workers exit the high-risk confirmed zone. They doff their contaminated PPE under careful supervision. They exit into the low-risk area and shower before leaving the clinic.

Disposing of infectious waste must be managed correctly during treatment and after the death of an Ebola patient. Each patient produces thirty to forty times the amount of medical waste than other patients do. PPE makes up much of that disposable waste because health-care workers can wear it only once. Waste also includes items used in caring for patients, such as linen, clothing, towels, privacy drapes, and bodily fluids. After patients recover—or die—assistants take the waste to a burn pit and incinerate it. Whatever cannot be burned must be disinfected. This includes plastic-covered mattresses and glass and metal objects. According to the CDC, the Ebola virus can remain infectious on dry surfaces such as countertops for several hours. The virus is infectious for several days in body fluids at room temperature (such as a puddle of blood left on a table).

The International Medical Corps (IMC) is a private nonprofit organization that works to save lives and relieve suffering around the world. IMC is another aid organization that built and staffed Ebola

A medical worker wearing protective gear disinfects himself after burning clothes worn by Ebola patients at a Doctors Without Borders facility in Monrovia. Ebola patients' clothing is considered dangerous medical waste.

treatment centers in West Africa. Lara Logan, a South African journalist, visited an IMC clinic in rural Liberia near the border with Guinea. Logan and her team traveled from Monrovia into the country along dirt roads pitted by potholes and puddles of water. The team stopped at several checkpoints during the long trip. Volunteers took everyone's temperature and washed them and their vehicles down with chlorinated water when they left.

She described her visit in a television news show aired in November 2014 on CBS's *60 Minutes*. "At the end of a dirt road, on the grounds of an old leper colony, we arrived after a five-hour drive at the International Medical Corps' Ebola treatment unit and were hosed down again," Logan said of her experience. "It's a one-disease hospital with fifty beds and a staff of nearly two hundred, run by US doctor Pranav Shetty, who trained in emergency medicine at UCLA [University of California, Los Angeles]."

The clinic that workers hacked out of the forest is the size of a football field. Gravel covers the ground, and the smell of chlorine fills the air. Blue tents that hold the patient wards and administrative offices dot the landscape. White plastic chairs provide seating for patients and for those awaiting the results of their Ebola tests. Orange mesh netting separates suspected-patient tents from confirmed-patient tents. Pans of chlorine and water spigots divide the sections.

During Logan's visit, a little boy named William who had Ebola sat in the sunshine outside a tent. His father—who had recovered from Ebola and was believed to be immune—gave William sips of water from a red plastic cup. A battery-powered radio and bottles of water rested on a table. Other patients who felt well enough to be outside sat nearby. The sickest ones rested on cots inside the tents. An ambulance (a pickup truck wrapped in orange plastic) pulled into the treatment center with a new patient destined for the suspected ward.

On the day Logan visited, the confirmed ward held about twenty patients. Many of the patients she met died. The cemetery was located at the end of a path through the trees. Gravediggers stabbed shovels into the red earth, adding new graves to the rows already in place. By the end of Logan's visit, more than sixty graves stretched beneath the trees, each marked by handwritten signs that listed a beloved person's name, date of birth, and date of death.

# Burying the Dead

The bodies of people who have died from Ebola are highly contagious in the hours and days after death. Researchers reported in February 2015 that Ebola viruses live in and on a corpse up to seven days. Everyone coming into contact with the corpse or its fluids is at extreme risk for getting Ebola. The WHO estimates that one-fifth of Ebola infections occur during burials. Special United Nations envoy Dr. David Nabarro said, "The commonest way in which people are getting Ebola is through the rituals that take place when somebody is buried, particularly the important cleansing and touching that goes on." Tradition in Guinea, Liberia, and Sierra Leone calls for family members to wash and dress bodies in clean clothing, to kiss them, and to embrace them as a way of saying good-bye. Friends and neighbors visit to express their grief and respect and to lay their hands on the dead person's body. After wrapping a body in a cloth or straw mat, people lower it into the ground. Family members often give away the person's personal property, which may be infected with Ebola.

All these activities associated with burial greatly increase the risk of infection. Health-care workers say people who have died from Ebola should be buried promptly and without touching them without PPE to decrease the risk of infection. Yet family members want to honor their age-old traditions. These conflicting goals sometimes

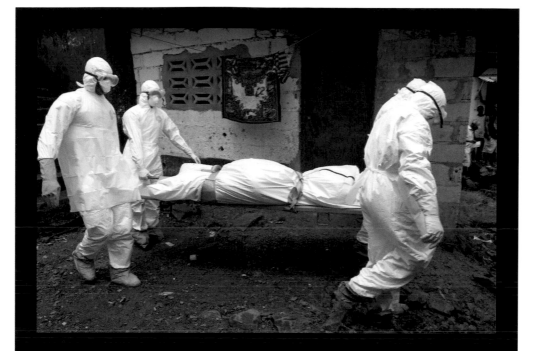

A Red Cross medical team in Monrovia transports the corpse of an Ebola patient. Upon death, each Ebola patient's body is placed in a plastic body bag. Anyone who works with the body after death—including during a funeral procession and the burial or cremation itself—must wear protective gear.

created mistrust and anger between West Africans and foreign health-care workers.

The WHO worked with anthropologists—people who study human culture—to develop burial rituals that are both safe and that meet West African cultural needs. The WHO team partnered with the International Federation of Red Cross and Red Crescent Societies (IFRC) and religious organizations to design new burial practices. Elhadj As Sy, the secretary-general of the IFRC said, "We safely, respectfully and in a dignified manner, accompany our deceased fellow human beings and help to prepare them, in accordance with their cultures, for their last resting places."

## DOGS AT RISK?

In 2014 Spanish nursing assistant Maria Teresa Romero Ramos developed Ebola after caring for two Spanish missionaries in a hospital in Madrid, Spain. The missionaries had contracted Ebola while working with Ebola patients in West Africa. Ramos was admitted to the hospital and recovered. Her husband was quarantined. He did not get sick and was released. Viewed as a potential risk for passing Ebola to people, their dog, Excalibur, was condemned to death and quickly put down by Spanish authorities. Nearly four hundred thousand people signed a petition to save Excalibur's life, without success. After the dog's death, Twitter posts using the hashtag #RIPExcalibur circulated throughout Spain. Thousands called for the health minister—who blamed Ramos for catching Ebola—to resign. Later, he publicly apologized and then resigned.

A few months later, US nurse Nina Pham was hospitalized in Dallas, Texas. She had contracted Ebola after caring for Thomas Duncan, an Ebola patient who died in Dallas. Veterinarians quarantined her dog, Bentley.

Ebola antibodies have been found in dogs, showing they had been exposed to Ebola. However, in 2014 the CDC said, "In the current epidemic and in previous Ebola outbreaks, exposure to dogs is not a risk factor for human infections." The CDC developed guidelines on managing dogs and cats belonging to Ebola victims. After being quarantined and monitored, much as a human contact of an Ebola patient would be, the animal is released after twenty-one days. American media widely publicized Pham's reunion with her dog (right) after she left the hospital.

Christianity and Islam are the main religions in West Africa. New burial protocols, therefore, needed to include instructions for both Muslim and Christian burials. The WHO team established burial teams made up of people trained in the safe handling of highly contagious bodies. The process of recruiting and training people for the burial teams was well under way by December 2014. The Reverend Monsignor Robert J. Vitillo of the Catholic charity Caritas Internationalis said, "Giving the family an opportunity to view the body of the deceased, ensuring that the grave is appropriately labelled, and allowing religious leaders to offer prayers . . . these are important incentives for encouraging families to find strength in their faith, and to keep other family members safe from becoming infected."

Sprays of disinfecting chlorinated water replace ritual washing of the corpse. Family members have the opportunity to look at their loved one for the last time before health-care workers close the plastic body bag in which the body is placed for transport and burial or cremation. The funeral procession and the burial itself occur with burial teams clothed in protective gear. The WHO believes that achieving an acceptable balance between necessary sanitary operations and cultural needs helps to reduce conflict between local communities and health workers.

However, even with new burial programs in place, some communities in Guinea, Liberia, and Sierra Leone believe the spirit of the departed requires traditional burial practices. The United Nations reported in February 2015 that secret burials were still occurring and were thwarting efforts to contain and end the Ebola epidemic.

A mother and her child in a classroom used as an Ebola isolation ward in Monrovia, Liberia. Patients with suspected or probable cases of Ebola are isolated from other patients while they await diagnostic results. Confirmed cases of Ebola are also separated from others. Isolation is a key protocol for containing the spread of the deadly disease.

# CHAPTER FIVE

# As the World Watched

Today, I ask the Congress to consider the enclosed emergency appropriations request for Fiscal Year 2015 that includes $6.18 billion to implement a comprehensive strategy to contain and end the Ebola outbreak. . . . My foremost priority is to protect the health and safety of Americans. . . . The best way to prevent additional cases at home will be to contain and eliminate the epidemic at its source in Africa.

—US president Barack Obama, 2014

**It took months for the world** to recognize that the 2014 Ebola outbreak in West Africa differed from smaller outbreaks of the past. Doctors Without Borders was the first organization to respond to the mounting Ebola crisis in West Africa. Even though fewer than 150 cases of Ebola had been identified by April 2014, the organization predicted an epidemic such as the world had never seen.

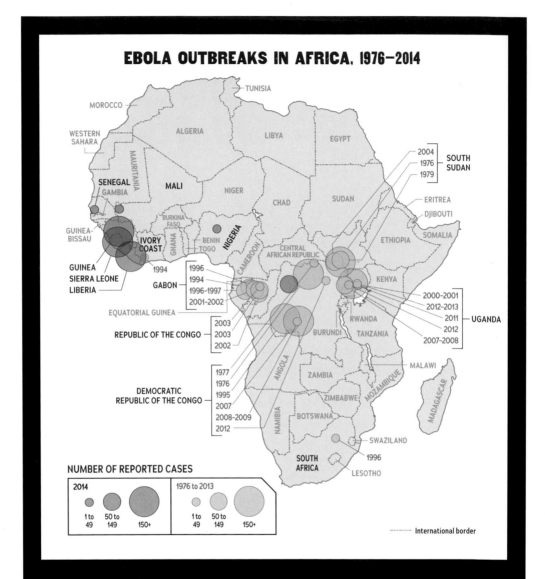

## EBOLA OUTBREAKS IN AFRICA, 1976–2014

TUNISIA

MOROCCO

WESTERN SAHARA

ALGERIA

LIBYA

EGYPT

MAURITANIA

SENEGAL
GAMBIA

MALI

NIGER

CHAD

SUDAN

2004
1976
1979

SOUTH SUDAN

ERITREA

DJIBOUTI

GUINEA-BISSAU

BURKINA FASO

GHANA

BENIN
TOGO

NIGERIA

CAMEROON

CENTRAL AFRICAN REPUBLIC

ETHIOPIA

SOMALIA

IVORY COAST

GUINEA
SIERRA LEONE
LIBERIA

1994

GABON

1996
1994
1996–1997
2001–2002

EQUATORIAL GUINEA

KENYA

2000–2001
2012–2013
2011
2012
2007–2008

UGANDA

REPUBLIC OF THE CONGO

2003
2003
2002

RWANDA

BURUNDI

TANZANIA

DEMOCRATIC REPUBLIC OF THE CONGO

1977
1976
1995
2007
2008–2009
2012

ANGOLA

ZAMBIA

ZIMBABWE

MALAWI

MOZAMBIQUE

MADAGASCAR

NAMIBIA

BOTSWANA

SOUTH AFRICA

SWAZILAND

1996

LESOTHO

### NUMBER OF REPORTED CASES

2014

1 to 49    50 to 149    150+

1976 to 2013

1 to 49    50 to 149    150+

- - - - - International border

This map highlights outbreaks of Ebola across the African continent through 2014. As of late summer 2015, the virus has killed nearly 11,300 people in Guinea, Sierra Leone, and Liberia alone. Suspected, probable, and confirmed cases of Ebola in those countries total roughly 27,700 cases. For more information about new cases, check the WHO website at http://apps.who.int/ebola/ebola-situation-reports.

The WHO disagreed. "This is relatively small still," WHO spokesperson Gregory Hartl said on April 1, 2014. "The biggest outbreaks have been over four hundred cases. Ebola already causes enough concern and we need to be very careful about how we characterize something which is up until now, an outbreak with sporadic cases." A journalist said the WHO was in denial, too snarled in red tape to recognize the pending disaster.

By June of that year, Doctors Without Borders was describing the outbreak as totally out of control. "There needs to be a real political commitment that this is a very big emergency," Bart Janssens of Doctors Without Borders said. "Otherwise, it will continue to spread, and for sure it will spread to more countries." He accused nations of not recognizing the gravity of the situation. He criticized the WHO for not doing more to inspire leaders to act. And his assessment was accurate.

During 2014 Ebola was found in Liberia, Guinea, Sierra Leone, Mali, and Nigeria. Thousands of people were dying, patients and medical workers alike. Health-care workers and missionaries from the affected countries and the United States, Spain, France, Germany, Great Britain, Norway, Scotland, and Switzerland became ill after caring for Ebola patients.

The virus was on the move. On August 8, 2014, the WHO finally declared the Ebola outbreak a global health emergency. How far would Ebola go? How fast would it spread?

# FEAR IN THE UNITED STATES

In the United States, fear was more contagious than Ebola itself. Parents pulled kids from schools. A passenger showed up at Dulles Airport near Washington, DC, dressed in a homemade hazmat suit, a full-length body covering made of plastic complete with hood and face mask. Louisiana banned thirty Ebola experts from attending an infectious disease conference in New Orleans because they'd been to West Africa. Parents demanded a Maine teacher be quarantined simply because she had visited Dallas, site of the first US Ebola death. Dozens of self-published Ebola survival guides flooded online booksellers. A Texas college refused to admit Nigerian applicants. A major US news organization said all air travel from West Africa should be banned.

An editorial in the *New England Journal of Medicine* compared the wave of Ebola paranoia that arose in the United States in 2014 to similar paranoia when HIV/AIDS was first identified in the early 1980s. During the 1980s and 1990s, some US public schools banned HIV-positive children. The editorial made reference to a 1986 piece by author William F. Buckley, who proposed in the *New York Times* that people with AIDS should be tattooed. Politicians called for the quarantine of all HIV-positive people. People with HIV faced discrimination in employment and housing. The editorial said of Ebola, "History is repeating itself as the irrational, punitive measures deployed in the AIDS epidemic thirty years ago are revived for another disease, this time a rare hemorrhagic fever."

By August 2015, only a handful of Ebola cases had surfaced in the United States. Yet according to a poll conducted by the Harvard School of Public Health at the height of the epidemic, more than half of Americans worried there would be a large outbreak of Ebola in the United States within the next year. More than one-third were concerned that they or someone in their families would get Ebola. Most Americans understood that Ebola is transmitted by contact with body fluids of an infected person. Even so, the same poll showed that 85 percent of Americans believed they could also get Ebola from people who were sneezing or coughing.

Some experts blamed print media and television for writing overly dramatic stories about Ebola. "Obviously, our fears have little to do with the things that might actually kill us," medical journalist Paul Waldman

In October 2014, a protester in front of the White House in Washington, DC, holds a "Stop the Flights" sign to express his support of a travel ban to stop flights to the United States from Ebola-stricken nations. At the time, the CDC had issued a warning against nonessential travel to Guinea, Sierra Leone, and Liberia. Travelers from affected countries who exhibit symptoms of possible Ebola infection may be prevented from boarding US planes and be restricted from traveling for a twenty-one-day watch period.

wrote in a 2014 article in the *Washington Post*. "We spend time and money worrying about the dramatic, unusual events like terrorism or infectious diseases, but don't think about things like car accidents (not to mention heart disease) that are much more likely to strike."

The Presidential Commission for the Study of Bioethical Issues issued a report in February 2015 that criticized the early US response to Ebola. "Americans focused on their own almost nonexistent risk of catching Ebola from travelers instead of pressing to help the truly affected nations," it said.

Consider this: between 5 and 20 percent of Americans get the flu each year. Between three thousand and forty-nine thousand people die annually of flu-related complications. Yet fewer than half of all Americans choose to receive the recommended vaccination to help prevent flu. Flu or Ebola? Which is the average American more likely to get? Which one should we really worry about the most?

## Ebola in the United States

As of July 2015, American hospitals had treated nearly a dozen people with Ebola. Eight were health-care workers who contracted Ebola while caring for patients in Africa or in the United States. One was a US cameraman on assignment in Liberia and one who was treated at the National Institutes of Health Clinical Center, the NIH's hospital in Bethesda, Maryland, chose to remain anonymous. A Liberian named Thomas Duncan traveled from West Africa to visit friends and family in Dallas. He did not realize he was infected with Ebola. Of these people, all but two recovered.

After Thomas Duncan entered the United States with an undiagnosed case of Ebola, President Obama asked health officials to develop better screening measures to prevent such a thing from happening again. The CDC and Homeland Security's Customs and Border Protection Department began screening incoming passengers at US airports. Everyone who has been to Liberia, Sierra Leone, or Guinea is required to fly into one of five designated US airports: JFK in New York City; Dulles near Washington, DC; Newark Liberty in Newark, New Jersey; O'Hare in Chicago, Illinois; or Hartsfield in Atlanta, Georgia.

On arrival, public health officials measure the passengers' temperatures and question them about symptoms. The passengers are required to take their temperatures for twenty-one days—the incubation period for Ebola. (The incubation period is the time between becoming infected and developing symptoms.) Travelers with no symptoms and who have not been exposed to Ebola may continue their travel as planned. They are connected with a state or local health department at their final destination for continued monitoring. People who have a fever or other symptoms or who have been exposed to Ebola receive additional screening. Depending on their risk category, travelers may be allowed to continue, may be followed up by the local health department, or may be taken to a local hospital. Airports screened 993 passengers in the first month. Seven were ill, but none had Ebola.

The governors of New Jersey, New York, and Connecticut decreed in October 2014 that all travelers from Liberia, Guinea, and Sierra Leone be monitored and/or quarantined for at least twenty-one days, even if they had no previous contact with Ebola patients. This included health-care workers as well as tourists and businesspeople.

While the CDC did not ban travel to West Africa, it issued a Level 3 Warning—its highest level—in November. It advised US citizens against nonessential travel to Sierra Leone, Guinea, and Liberia because of Ebola. The CDC lowered its warning for travel to Liberia to Level 2—practice enhanced precautions—as cases declined greatly in the spring of 2015.

Criticism of these moves came from various quarters. "Stopping the entire world from traveling is not the solution to containing this outbreak," Dr. Isabelle Nuttall of the WHO said. "We know what is needed to stop this outbreak and it doesn't include banning people from traveling from West Africa to the US or Western Europe. Travel bans are detrimental and ineffective." Health experts at Harvard University warned that unnecessary quarantines might stop health-care workers from volunteering to work in Ebola-stricken countries.

At about the same time, Dallas nurses Nina Pham and Amber Vinson contracted Ebola while caring for Thomas Duncan. They were experienced nurses who had followed the hospital safety protocols in place at the time. Until then US health officials had believed that any hospital could safely handle Ebola patients. The infection of Pham and Vinson changed that. "It is unreasonable to expect every acute-care hospital in the nation to have the capacity for treating Ebola patients," Peter Hotez of the National School of Tropical Medicine in Houston, Texas, said. In response, state health officials chose fifty-five hospitals across the United States as Ebola treatment centers. Staff in those hospitals received specialized training in how to safely care for Ebola patients.

The CDC published new recommendations for the care of Ebola patients in US hospitals, emergency rooms, and in outpatient settings. The organization tightened its recommendations on donning and doffing PPE. It developed stringent protocols for cleaning hospital rooms, handling infectious waste, and for the collection and transport of laboratory specimens such as blood. The CDC also developed a three-day training course for health-care personnel traveling to West Africa to care for Ebola patients.

## THE INTERNATIONAL RESPONSE

The United States joined at least thirty other nations in providing funds and health-care workers to deal with the Ebola crisis in West Africa. According to one source, the United States pledged to send $2.3 billion and twenty-two hundred health-care workers. It also sent about four thousand members of the US military to build clinics.

The CDC also sent staff. For example, one of Dr. Karlyn Beer's jobs in Liberia was to collect and manage data. "My deployment started at 8:00 am on a Saturday, when two other Epidemic Intelligence Service Officers and I got off the plane in Monrovia. We made it to the hotel in time to join our CDC colleagues for breakfast, put our bags in our rooms, and hop in a van to the ministry of health [MoH]," she said.

"There was a backlog of lab results to enter into the electronic data management system. The MoH building is three stories, surrounded by a big fence, and looks like an old school building. Cars with 'Let's fight Ebola' decals were parked in the dirt driveway. We spent the day in a room where computers were set up on tables, classroom-style, and cables crisscrossed the floor. The MoH had a dedicated staff who worked day in and day out to record Ebola case information, despite little or no pay. They kept things fun by singing to Nigerian pop music on the radio."

Many countries joined the United States in offering aid to West Africa. Great Britain pledged $453 million and 1,085 workers. China pledged $122.5 million and one thousand workers. Cuba, a poor country with a very high doctor-to-patient ratio, pledged five hundred health-care workers. The Bill & Melinda Gates Foundation pledged $50 million, and the World Bank (an international financial institution that provides loans to developing countries), $518 million. The US-based Christian organization Samaritan's Purse shipped tons of supplies including food, water, medicine, and medical supplies to West Africa. It built and staffed Ebola treatment centers. Doctors Without Borders also sent tons of medical supplies. The organization deployed hundreds of health-care workers; hired thousands more locally; and built and maintained Ebola treatment centers in Liberia, Sierra Leone, and Guinea.

Was that enough? According to the United Nations, the world needed to do much more because the virus was still outpacing response activities. Dr. Jim Yong Kim, president of the World Bank, said that a shortage of trained medical personnel in West Africa was hampering efforts to bring the epidemic under control. He called for thousands more health-care workers to be sent to the area.

Doctors Without Borders had warned the world for months about the dangers of the 2014 Ebola epidemic. While recognizing some progress had been made by December 2014, the group said, "On the whole . . . the response to this rapidly-changing epidemic has so far been inadequate. Instead of the well-controlled, comprehensive and expertly-staffed intervention [we] called for ninety days ago, actual efforts have been sluggish and patchy, falling dangerously short of expectations."

In a December 2014 briefing paper, Doctors Without Borders pointed out areas of concern that needed to be addressed at that time:

1. The international response to Ebola has been slow and hampered by bottlenecks in staffing. Training health-care workers to safely treat Ebola patients takes time and resources. Countries need to not only send money and build clinics. They must provide the necessary training as well.

2. In Liberia, Sierra Leone, and Guinea, major gaps exist in health-care facilities. For example, new clinics have been built in major cities, while rural areas are short of beds.

3. International aid is not adapting quickly enough to a rapidly changing situation. Resources are often allocated to the wrong location and for the wrong purpose.

## A Society in Crisis

With increasing international assistance, experts predicted that the Ebola epidemic in West Africa would come to an end. However, as devastating as Ebola was, other major challenges faced Liberia, Guinea, and Sierra Leone. These countries had struggled to recover from decades of civil war that had lasted until 1999 in Guinea, 2002 in Sierra Leone, and 2003 in Liberia. Ebola wiped out much of that postwar progress and plunged the countries into crisis. In addition, other more common diseases plague these nations.

# FATU KEKULA SAVES HER FAMILY

Dr. William Fischer, who worked in Guinea for several weeks in 2014, said of PPE, "I honestly believe you could probably wear a trash bag and be safe." It's unlikely that Liberian nursing student Fatu Kekula read Dr. Fischer's words, which were published in the *Los Angeles Times*. Yet the twenty-two-year-old nursing student did just that.

Fatu Kekula's father contracted Ebola in a hospital in Kakata (a small city not far from Monrovia) but came home thinking it was some other illness. Kekula took her father to three hospitals in Monrovia, which turned him away because they were full. She then took him to another hospital in Kakata, where doctors said he had typhoid fever and sent him home. He soon infected Kekula's mother, her sister, and her fourteen-year-old cousin. Kekula had no other choice but to take care of her family at home. She consulted the family doctor by phone because he would not come to the house. She received medications and intravenous supplies from a local clinic.

For two weeks, Kekula operated a one-woman Ebola hospital. She knew the importance of donning protective gear, so several times each day, she put black plastic trash bags over her socks and knotted them over her calves. She put on rubber boots and added another bag over them. She wrapped her hair in stockings and then tied a plastic bag like a scarf over her head. She then donned a raincoat, four pairs of gloves, and a mask. She saved her father, mother, and sister without becoming infected with Ebola herself, although her cousin died.

After CNN ran Kekula's story, a crowdfunding group raised $40,000 to cover some of her expenses to complete her nursing education. Emory University in Atlanta awarded Kekula a partial scholarship to the university's nursing school. She started school there in January 2015. "These things that I have learned here I am going to take back to my fellow nurses," Kekula said in a 2015 television interview. "I love to care for people. I love to save lives."

For example, Drs. Peter Piot and Jeremy Farrar wrote in the *New England Journal of Medicine*, "These health system effects [overwhelmed and dysfunctional health-care systems] will only worsen as the [Ebola] epidemic progresses. West Africa will see much more suffering and many more deaths during childbirth and from malaria, tuberculosis, HIV–AIDS, enteric and respiratory illnesses, diabetes, cancer, cardiovascular disease, and mental health [problems] during and after the Ebola epidemic."

The crisis in Ebola-affected regions was about more than health care. Governments shut down and canceled elections. Officials slowed or stopped travel between affected areas. Employment fell by nearly half as businesses and markets closed in fear of Ebola. Incomes plummeted. Families and farmers who might have harvested and sold their crops fell ill or died from the virus. Or they simply could not get enough help to harvest their crops. Food became expensive and scarce. For example, the price of rice—an important staple in the region—rose by 40 percent.

The World Food Programme (the food assistance branch of the United Nations) estimated in November 2014 that 200,000 people had problems getting food because of the Ebola epidemic. In January 2015, the World Bank reported that two-thirds of households could not get enough rice to meet their family's needs. The organization said it needed $1 billion to help Liberia, Sierra Leone, and Guinea. Health officials predicted that between 750,000 and 1.4 million people would lose access to affordable food by March 2015 because of the wider impact of Ebola.

Dr. Karlyn Beer saw proof of these problems during her deployment to Liberia. "I visited several border crossings to find out whether people, products, and potentially Ebola could cross into neighboring countries," she says. "One border crossing is a river that separates Liberia from Ivory Coast. Normally, this crossing has a floating barge that carries large trucks and other vehicles between countries. But

As Ebola spread across West Africa, families fled affected areas, creating a refugee crisis, particularly as nations began to close their borders to prevent the spread of the disease. The occupants of this vehicle are fleeing Senegal, where Ebola broke out in the summer of 2014.

the barge had been grounded on the Ivory Coast side since the Ebola epidemic began and governments closed the borders. Because of border closings like this one, fewer foods and other goods arrived in Liberia, which drove prices up."

In addition to economic problems, survivors faced stigma as family and friends feared that survivors still carried Ebola. Some people suspected that people who had recovered from Ebola were witches. As a result, many survivors had problems finding work or a place to live. Taxi drivers refused them rides, and barbers would only cut their hair while wearing gloves. Achille Guemou, a doctor in Guinea who survived Ebola said, "Before Ebola, I was somebody. I was the local doctor. People used to knock at my door all day seeking advice. Now, they avoid me in the street."

Mami Bienda *(left)* and Lassana Gabana *(right)* both survived Ebola. Many survivors live with post-Ebola syndrome, which includes vision problems, body aches, headaches, and fatigue. Others deal with the grief and loneliness from having lost family members to the disease. Survivors left with no source of income struggle financially. Some are stigmatized as witches for having survived the dread disease. With help from government and international aid organizations, communities are training counselors and providing educational materials to help individuals and communities recover from Ebola.

Ebola orphans have fared better. According to the United Nations Children's Fund, known as UNICEF, Ebola left more than sixteen thousand orphans. Extended family members or local families typically took them in. Andrew Brooks speaking for UNICEF in February 2015 said, "There were fears that stigma around Ebola would isolate the orphaned children . . . but that has, luckily, not materialized. The stigma and the fear have not completely disappeared, but the bonds of kinship and traditional relations have proven to be stronger, which was why families had taken kids in."

## Post-Ebola Syndrome

Doctors have also identified a new threat: post-Ebola syndrome. At least half of all Ebola survivors have developed vision problems that in some cases progress to blindness. For example, Dr. Ian Crozier is a US physician who developed Ebola while working in Sierra Leone in 2014. Although Dr. Crozier had recovered from Ebola by October, he became nearly blind in one eye. Researchers at Emory University Hospital in Atlanta were shocked to discover living viruses inside his eye two months later. Until then, no one had known that Ebola could enter the eye.

Other survivors experience muscle and joint pain, chest pain, headaches, hearing loss, and fatigue. Symptoms can last a long time, making it difficult or impossible to return to work. "We need to understand why these symptoms persist, whether they are caused by the disease or treatment, or perhaps the heavy disinfection," Dr. Margaret Nanyonga of the WHO said.

The world watched the Ebola epidemic play out in West Africa. It took a few months, but the world began offering help—health-care workers, medical supplies, building materials, and money. All were important. All were needed, but perhaps none more so than health-care workers as they worked to understand and treat Ebola and the post-Ebola symptom.

## PERSON OF THE YEAR

Each year *Time* magazine names a "Person of the Year." The person (group, idea, or object) that *Time* chooses must have strongly influenced events of the previous year, for better or for worse. Past issues have featured presidents and popes, leaders of technology and science. For its 2014 person of the year, *Time* chose the health-care workers they named the Ebola Fighters. Editor Nancy Gibbs wrote, "The rest of the world can sleep at night because a group of men and women are willing to stand and fight. For tireless acts of courage and mercy, for buying the world time to boost its defenses, for risking, for persisting, for sacrificing and saving, the Ebola Fighters are *TIME*'s 2014 Person of the Year."

Ebola vaccine trials began in Monrovia in early February 2015. Participants include healthy adults as well as health-care workers, contact tracers, members of burial teams, and others at high risk of contracting the disease.

# CHAPTER SIX

# DIAGNOSING THE FUTURE

The unprecedented scale of the current Ebola outbreak in West Africa has intensified efforts to develop safe and effective vaccines, which may play a role in bringing this epidemic to an end, and undoubtedly will be critically important in preventing future large outbreaks.

—Anthony S. Fauci, MD, director, National Institute of Allergy and Infectious Diseases, 2014

**How do you decide which patients** with Ebola will receive an experimental medication that might cure them—or kill them? Would you want to take a drug that had only been tested on monkeys? Are poorly educated people with no knowledge of modern medicine capable of signing the legal consent forms authorizing doctors to try out new drugs on them? Drugs that may kill them? The world first learned about Ebola in 1976. Why wasn't there a vaccine to prevent it or medications to cure it in 2014? These are a few of the ethical questions that world health leaders grappled with at the height of the Ebola epidemic.

Americans Dr. Kent Brantly and Nancy Writebol fell ill with Ebola in July 2014 while working in a clinic in a suburb of Monrovia. The organization they worked for, Samaritan's Purse, contacted the CDC to ask if a drug was available to help them. The CDC put the group in touch with the National Institutes of Health staff working in West Africa. The NIH knew of a scarce experimental medication called ZMapp that had cured monkeys with Ebola, but the drug had never been given to people.

"Our staff in Liberia knew about the [ZMapp] research," said Dr. Anthony Fauci, director of the NIH's National Institute of Allergy and Infectious Diseases. "The physicians in charge of the patients' care made a risk-benefit decision. The risk [of harmful side effects from the drug] was less than the potential benefit." So both Americans received ZMapp in Africa before the United States evacuated them and brought them back home.

Brantly and Writebol signed informed consent forms to receive ZMapp. These consents ensure that people taking an experimental drug know all the risks of doing so, up to and including death. However, some people criticized health officials for not offering ZMapp to sick Africans. Yet what might have happened if two Liberians who were not well-informed medically instead of two Americans had received the ZMapp and died? "It would have been the front-page screaming headline: 'Africans used as guinea pigs for American drug company's medicine,'" said Dr. Salim S. Abdool Karim, director of Caprisa, an AIDS research center in South Africa.

Journalists debated the issue in major publications. Author Harriet Washington wrote an opinion-editorial piece for CNN. "Why didn't Dr. Sheik Umar Khan, the chief Sierra Leone physician who died while treating Ebola patients, receive [ZMapp]?" she asked. "Because another method of determining who gets medications is at work here—the drearily familiar stratification [to classify people by their socioeconomic class] of access to a drug based on economic resources and being a

Westerner. . . . Informal medical networks, which Africans lack, connect well-to-do Westerners with information and drugs."

Laura Seay, assistant professor of government at Maine's Colby College and an expert on African politics, felt differently. Writing for the *Washington Post*, she said, "The first and most important principle of ethical research is that the subjects (in this case, Ebola patients) are able to give meaningful informed consent. . . . Can someone who is gravely ill and who has never heard of the concept of "informed consent" really fully consider the implications of taking a drug like ZMapp? Could he or she feel coerced [forced] because foreign doctors are the ones asking for consent? . . . Add to this the dilemmas of cross-cultural communication, where misunderstanding is as likely as not, and it is very likely that "consent" becomes meaningless in the context in which the Ebola outbreak is happening."

In the end, ethical standards of medical care called for a fully informed consent. But the medication's success in treating Brantly and Writebol spurred new research. The rush was on to produce more ZMapp and to discover other medications to treat Ebola. Testing of ZMapp among Ebola patients began in 2015 and was expected to last into 2016. Perhaps even more important, however, the world needed a vaccine to prevent Ebola, as well as medications to cure it.

# Vaccines to Prevent Ebola

Vaccines help to prevent specific diseases. For example, children routinely receive measles vaccinations. Vaccinated children who come into contact with a person who has measles are unlikely to get sick, and therefore measles almost never occurs in the United States. While nearly 160 Americans developed measles during an outbreak in 2014–2015, the vast majority had never received the measles vaccine. Vaccines stimulate the immune system to produce antibodies against organisms such as the virus that causes measles. The measles virus—and all viruses—carry molecules on their cells called antigens. If antibodies in the immune system of a vaccinated person detect measles antigens, the antibodies destroy the virus. Vaccines "train" the immune system to recognize and destroy the foreign invaders.

However, when the 2014 Ebola epidemic began, there was no vaccine to prevent it. When the Ebola virus entered the body, the immune system had no antibodies to recognize it or to fight it. Instead, the virus was free to attack the immune system. An Ebola vaccine was urgently needed.

By late 2014, several vaccines were in clinical trials—the standardized scientific method for testing new vaccines and medications. Several experimental vaccines showed success in preventing Ebola in animals and were moved to human trials. The first phase of a clinical trial tells researchers if the vaccine is safe for people. Investigators also learn if it stimulates antibodies against Ebola in this phase.

Several nations tested different Ebola vaccines. For example, in late December 2014, the British medical journal *Lancet* reported success of phase 1 clinical trials of an Ebola vaccine, which involves giving healthy people a vaccine to see if it is safe. The trial included tests of a new vaccine for the closely related Marburg virus as well. In the trial, 108 healthy volunteers in Uganda agreed to participate after signing informed consents. Doctors randomly assigned each person to receive an injection of the Ebola vaccine, the Marburg vaccine, both, or a placebo (an inert medication, typically salt water).

The vaccines proved to be both safe and effective. They stimulated the development of antibodies to fight a future Ebola or Marburg infection. "This is the first study to show comparable safety and immune response of an experimental Ebola vaccine in an African population," Dr. Julie Ledgerwood from the US National Institute of Allergy and Infectious Diseases said. "This is especially encouraging because those at

# CLINICAL TRIALS

A clinical trial involves research to discover how new medications work in humans. A principal investigator, who is often a medical doctor or PhD scientist, leads the study. The trials have a research team that includes doctors, nurses, social workers, and other health-care professionals. New prescription medications and vaccines go through clinical trials, the most rigorous type of study, before they are legally approved for use among the general public. These are the phases of a clinical trial:

**Phase 1:** Is the treatment safe? The drug is given for the first time to a small number of healthy volunteers to determine its safety, dosage, and side effects.

**Phase 2:** Does the treatment work? The drug is given to a larger group of people to determine if it is both safe and effective for the condition it is intended to treat.

**Phase 3:** How does this treatment compare with existing treatments? This phase involves thousands of people taking the drug at multiple medical centers. It confirms the effectiveness of the drug, monitors side effects, and compares the drug with other medications used to treat the same condition. These studies are randomized and double-blinded, which means that neither the patient nor the researcher knows who receives the medication and who receives a placebo.

**Phase 4:** Are there other potential uses for this treatment, and what are the long-term adverse effects? This phase may involve millions of people taking the drug for years to identify any long-term side effects. During this phase of a trial, doctors are legally allowed to use the medication for other purposes than the one for which it was originally intended.

greatest risk of Ebola live primarily in Africa." However, the antibodies lasted only a few months. Researchers planned to test a stronger vaccine.

The second phase of a clinical trial determines if the vaccine is effective at preventing Ebola. Some phase 2 trials of different vaccines began early in 2015. In January 2015, the NIH announced it would begin testing two different vaccines in Liberia. Six hundred volunteers would be split into three groups. Two groups would receive separate vaccines, while the third group would receive a placebo. If the vaccines proved safe, researchers would move to the next phase. In that phase, researchers planned to vaccinate about twenty-seven thousand people. The large number of volunteers would include people at risk for Ebola, such as health-care workers, burial teams, and communities with ongoing cases of Ebola. The trial would be double-blinded, meaning neither the volunteers nor the staff would know which vaccine would be given or if a volunteer received a placebo.

Testing of vaccines in Africa remains controversial, however. The World Health Organization launched clinical trials for experimental Ebola vaccines in March 2015 in Ghana, a West African nation free of Ebola. Ghana initially agreed to participate in phase 1 testing. In June

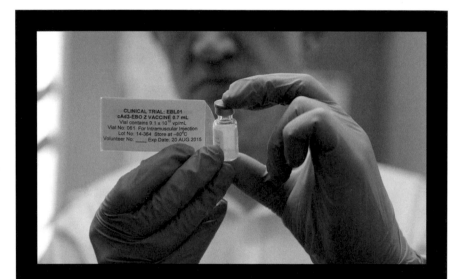

One of the experimental Ebola vaccines, cAd3-EBOZ *(above)*, delivers Ebola genetic material from the Ebola (formerly Zaire) strain of the virus, which caused the 2014 West African outbreak. Early results from a phase 1 trial of this vaccine showed that it initiated immune responses to the outer coat of the virus.

2015, government leaders in Ghana called for an end to the trials. "We have cases of malaria, cholera and HIV/AIDS among others. We need vaccines or remedies for these diseases," the leaders said. "Why should a country that is not threatened by Ebola risk the lives of its citizens for an unnecessary experiment? We would be grateful if the experiment is cancelled completely to prevent the use of innocent [Ghanaians] as guinea pigs." Ghanaian health minister Alex Segbefia suspended Ebola vaccine trials even though the Ghanaian Food and Drugs Authority warned that Ghana is close enough to the affected countries to be at risk for Ebola.

On July 31, 2015, the WHO announced that a new vaccine— called VSV-EBOV—appears to be 75 percent to 100 percent effective at preventing Ebola. This is an extremely promising development," said Dr. Margaret Chan, Director-General of WHO. "An effective vaccine will be another very important tool for both current and future Ebola outbreaks."

## Help from Survivors' Blood

People who survive Ebola have developed large numbers of Ebola antibodies in their blood. Doctors believe the blood of these survivors can help people who are sick with Ebola to recover. It takes the body about two weeks after a vaccination to produce antibodies. Getting a transfusion of blood from Ebola survivors is like getting an instant vaccine. Patients don't have to wait for their immune system to make antibodies.

Dr. Kent Brantly received a blood donation in Africa when he developed Ebola. After he fully recovered in the United States, he donated blood to three other patients, including Dallas nurse Nina Pham. Amber Vinson was the second Dallas nurse to contract Ebola from patient Thomas Duncan. After her recovery, she donated her blood to a Texas biotechnology firm that planned to develop an Ebola drug from her antibodies. "I'm one of the few people here in the States that can provide the blood for research," Vinson told a television reporter. "I want to do what I can to help. That's the 'nurse' part of me. It's a changing world, and this is a step I can take to help the next person out."

About 130 Ebola survivors in Guinea and 100 in Liberia agreed to donate their blood to help others. "This is not a simple intervention," said Alan Magill of the Bill & Melinda Gates Foundation, which funded the research in Guinea. "It requires complex tools and very skilled people." In the Gates trials, survivors donated blood at a mobile laboratory located inside a blue school bus parked in Conakry, Guinea. Technicians separated donor red blood cells from the plasma, the portion of blood that contains the valuable antibodies. They screened the blood to be sure the donor didn't have HIV or hepatitis. In some locations, health-care workers used a new method to treat the plasma to kill all bacteria or viruses that may be present to prevent accidental infections.

To receive the treatment, the patient and the donor must have the same blood types. Once the donor and recipient are matched, doctors give three doses of the antibody-rich plasma to the patient over four days. Researchers measure the level of Ebola antibodies in recipients' blood before and after they receive the antibodies. If the treatment succeeds, patients are expected to have higher levels of Ebola antibodies after receiving the plasma. Clinical trials of this procedure started in Africa in late December 2014 and looked promising.

## FINDING NEW MEDICATIONS FOR EBOLA

The FDA is the organization that ensures medications used in the United States are both safe and effective. As of July 2015, the FDA has not approved any medications to treat Ebola. However, as of early January 2015, several promising Ebola medications were in different stages of clinical trials.

Perhaps the best known of these experimental drugs is ZMapp. Dr. Kent Brantly and Nancy Writebol, who were infected with Ebola while working in Liberia, recovered after getting ZMapp. While they both recovered, researchers could not be sure it was the ZMapp that saved their lives or the advanced medical care they received in US hospitals.

ZMapp is developed in living plants that have been genetically altered. It carries three different antibodies. When injected into the bloodstream, two of the antibodies bind to the base of the Ebola virus and prevent it from entering cells in the body. If a virus cannot get into a cell, it cannot take over the cell and replicate. The third antibody (blue in the photo below) binds near the top of the virus and possibly acts as a beacon to summon the immune system to kick into action. It's time-consuming to make enough ZMapp for trials, but scientists are working on new methods to produce the required antibodies more quickly.

This model of ZMapp antibodies show the two that bind to the base of the Ebola virus *(shown in white above)* and prevent it from entering cells in the body. The third antibody binds near the top of the virus and possibly triggers the body's immune system to kick into action.

In South Dakota, cows are busy producing large amounts of Ebola antibodies in their blood plasma. Scientists have genetically modified the cows so they produce human antibodies, not bovine antibodies. In theory, each cow could produce up to one thousand doses of Ebola antibodies per month. The US Army Medical Research Institute of Infectious Diseases is working with a drug company on the project.

Other medications to treat Ebola are being developed and tested. These include the following:

- TKM-Ebola is an experimental drug that seems to prevent Ebola in lab monkeys. It targets three of Ebola's seven genes and prevents them from replicating. Human clinical trials are under way.

- Two experimental antiviral drugs called brincidofovir and favipiravir might prove useful for Ebola. These medications prevent viral replication once the virus enters a cell. The first was developed in the United States to treat cytomegalovirus and adenovirus infections. The second was made in Japan and seems to be effective against viruses that cause influenza, West Nile, and yellow fever. After testing in Guinea, health officials announced in February 2015 that favipiravir appears to speed the recovery of Ebola patients who have low to moderate levels of the virus in their blood. Dr. Bertrand Draguez, medical director of Doctors Without Borders, stressed that these results were preliminary. "Research into favipiravir, and into other potential treatments for EVD [Ebola virus disease], must be continued, and [Doctors Without Borders] is willing to play a role in these clinical trials," he said.

- Doctors sometimes try existing FDA-approved medications on new diseases. For example, a study led by the NIH and the Icahn School of Medicine in New York has identified fifty-three drugs that may help to prevent the Ebola virus from entering human cells and replicating there. Cancer drugs, antihistamines, antibiotics, and drugs used to treat depression have all blocked or partially blocked the Ebola virus from entering cells. In May 2015, researchers announced limited success with using well-established HIV drugs for Ebola. Further testing is required to determine if they are effective against the Ebola virus.

- Another company has worked on a medication to prevent shock, a fatal complication of Ebola. Called LB1148, it helps prevent the intestinal tract from leaking enzymes and bacteria into the bloodstream, which together lead to shock. LB1148 is a powder that is mixed with water and taken by mouth. The patient sips the 3-cup (700-milliliter) dose over twenty-four hours. The patient may receive three to ten doses of LB1148. It does not require refrigeration or sterile needles. This makes it easy and safe to administer in the difficult conditions of Ebola-stricken nations.

## NEW TESTS AND BETTER PPE

Tests for Ebola take hours or days to provide results. People exposed to Ebola must remain in quarantine until staff knows if a person is infected or not. Better, faster tests are needed. The most common test for Ebola is the polymerase chain reaction (PCR) test. It uses samples of a patient's blood or saliva and looks for tiny amounts of genetic material from the virus. It then makes enough copies of that material so that the virus can be more easily detected. While PCR is efficient, it takes several hours to complete, it's expensive (one hundred US dollars per test), and it can give a negative reading during the first three days a person is sick with Ebola. It is a complex test and requires trained laboratory scientists with specialized equipment.

Another test—the enzyme-linked immunosorbent assay (ELISA)—looks for Ebola antibodies in a patient's blood. It takes longer than three days for a patient to produce enough Ebola antibodies to detect. Doctors can also culture the patient's blood in living cells and use an electron microscope to look for Ebola viruses. These tests require highly trained personnel and specialized laboratory equipment. And culturing Ebola viruses is very dangerous for laboratory workers because exposure to infected blood can transmit the disease.

According to the WHO, the ideal test for Ebola would take place in a clinic without a lab, produce a result in thirty minutes, be inexpensive and easy to perform, and only require equipment that is portable and requires no electricity. In November 2014, the WHO challenged diagnostic companies to produce such a test as soon as possible. A better, faster test would more quickly identify Ebola patients and allow treatment of infected people to begin sooner.

Researchers at Wellcome Trust, an international health charity, planned to try a new test in an Ebola treatment center in Guinea. The test—six times faster than standard tests—is performed in a portable lab the size of a laptop computer. A solar panel with a backup power pack provides energy. The testing materials are dried pellets and do not need refrigeration, unlike most testing materials. The test detects the genetic material of the Ebola virus in about fifteen minutes. "A reliable, 15-minute test that can confirm cases of Ebola would be a key tool for effective management of the Ebola outbreak," Dr. Val Snewin of Wellcome Trust said. "It not only gives patients a better chance of survival, but it prevents transmission of the virus to other people."

The FDA has approved tests that can detect Ebola in an hour from saliva, blood, or urine samples. But the machines to run the tests are expensive, and each test costs nearly $200. In February 2015, the WHO approved a test called the ReEBOV Antigen Rapid Test. It involves putting a drop of blood on a test strip that contains Ebola antibodies. If Ebola antigens are present in the blood sample, a dark line appears on the test strip. Health-care workers could carry these testing materials to remote villages. They could test people in door-to-door campaigns in larger villages and towns. Airport screeners could use the tests to quickly identify a traveler with Ebola.

Researchers and health-care officials are also looking for better PPE. The ideal protective suit would be easy to don and doff, and it would not be as uncomfortably hot to wear as current PPE. That would allow health-care workers wearing PPE to spend more time with patients. In 2014 the US Agency for International Development staged the Ebola Grand Challenge to encourage researchers to come up with a better design. The agency received fifteen hundred entries.

International passenger screening for Ebola is taking place at various airports around the world. A first screening is to check a traveler's temperature, as in this photo from the international airport in Seoul, South Korea. Passengers may be asked if they have been near anyone with Ebola or if they have symptoms of the disease. Travelers suspected of having Ebola are taken to a hospital for isolation and observation.

A team from the prestigious Johns Hopkins University in Baltimore, Maryland, was one of three winners in the global competition. The Hopkins prototype design differs greatly from PPE currently in use. The zipper is in the back instead of in the front. Tabs allow the suit to fall off the wearer after pulling the tabs. Instead of a twenty-step doffing process, removal of the suit takes only six steps and less than one minute. A battery pack worn on a belt cools the workers by blowing dry, filtered air into the hood of the suit. This helps sweat evaporate from the skin, cooling the worker. The battery pack is recharged by a cell phone charger once the suit has been doffed. The suit will require intensive testing, however, before it is manufactured and delivered for use in the field.

In another innovative measure, the US Pentagon, headquarters of the US Department of Defense, has worked to develop a portable "Care Cube." This protective bubble puts the *patient* into the protective suit—which is like a tiny room—while the health-care worker stays outside. Everything needed to care for the patient for ten days is inside the cube. Health-care workers reach into the bubble to do their work, wearing protective isolation gloves. The cube provides ventilation in such a way as to protect those outside the cube from possible contamination.

# WHAT WENT WRONG?

In late January 2015, Dr. Margaret Chan, the director-general of the World Health Organization, publicly acknowledged that the WHO had been too slow to realize the importance of the outbreak and too slow to respond. "The Ebola outbreak points to the need for urgent change in three main areas," she said. "To rebuild and strengthen national and international emergency preparedness and response, to address the way new medical products are brought to market, and to strengthen the way WHO operates during emergencies."

As the Ebola crisis emerged in Liberia, army troops joined police to patrol the streets of Monrovia *(above)* and in other communities. The nation's president declared a state of emergency, limiting public gatherings, closing schools, and imposing mandatory leave for nonessential government employees. Police and soldiers also aided in contact tracing, delivering medical supplies, and closing borders.

In May 2015, the WHO issued a report that assessed its own response and the world's response to the Ebola epidemic. Findings suggest that the WHO and others did not respond as effectively as possible for reasons that included the following:

- The Ebola epidemic was the largest and most complex in history and put enormous strains on national and international response capacities, including the WHO's outbreak and emergency response structures.
- Other major global public health issues were competing for the WHO's attention, such as Middle East Respiratory Syndrome (MERS), polio, and avian influenza.

- Health-care systems in Liberia, Sierra Leone, and Guinea were fragile and struggling, allowing Ebola to spread rapidly.
- While traditional culture in West Africa such as funeral and burial customs contributed to the spread of the disease, culturally sensitive engagement with local peoples seldom occurred in the early stages of the epidemic. This led to mistrust of foreign aid workers.
- Early Ebola warnings from May through July 2014 from experts such as Doctors Without Borders were largely ignored by the WHO and other international organizations.

Laurie Garrett, Pulitzer Prize–winning medical journalist, wrote an article published in June 2015 in the prestigious magazine *Foreign Policy*. In the article, she cited the top two of the many mistakes the WHO made in its handling of the Ebola epidemic. The first was that the organization's leadership in its Swiss headquarters and in its regional office in Africa had ". . . concluded in late March 2014, that the Ebola outbreak in Guinea was winding down and that most of the infected individuals had been identified and were being monitored, so it was safe to withdraw international experts from the region. They were wrong." The virus soon spread from Guinea into Sierra Leone and Liberia.

The second mistake, Garrett says, "was Director-General Margaret Chan's decision to delay the formal declaration of a 'public health emergency of international concern' until August 8, 2014, by which time the virus was claiming lives in the cities of Conakry [Guinea], Freetown [Sierra Leone], and Monrovia [Liberia], and had spread to Nigeria." US and Spanish health-care workers had also become infected and were being treated in their home countries.

Doctors Without Borders remains one of the biggest critics of the WHO's and the world's response to the Ebola epidemic. "If a global pandemic were to strike tomorrow," said Dr. Joanne Liu, international president of Doctors Without Borders, "there is still no well-resourced, coordinated international response in place to kick in."

The G7, a group of leaders from seven major, wealthy nations, met in June 2015. The agenda included the world's response to Ebola. "The G7 leaders must recognize this gaping hole in our global health system and take concrete action to address it," Dr. Liu said, "or risk losing thousands of more lives in the next major epidemic." A press release about G7 activities at the meeting, however, offered nothing new. It merely stated the G7 countries need to fully fund their financial commitments and to carry out planned activities in an efficient and effective manner.

## THE BEGINNING OF THE END?

Will the 2014 Ebola epidemic come to an end? Or will small outbreaks continue to pop up in rural villages? Dr. Thomas Frieden, director of the CDC, visited West Africa in December 2014 to help health-care officials figure out how to find and isolate new Ebola cases more quickly. If that can't be done, Ebola may become a permanent disease in the region. "That's exactly the risk we face now," Dr. Frieden said, "that Ebola will simmer along, become endemic and be a problem for Africa and the world for years to come. As the weeks have gone by, we have been able to intervene faster [in Liberia]. We've found that we can stop outbreaks in weeks instead of months."

While Dr. David Nabarro, UN Special Envoy on Ebola, didn't feel completely confident in predicting the end of the epidemic, he saw signs of hope. In January 2015, he said, "The change in behavior that we've been hoping for, working for, anticipating, is now happening everywhere. The facilities to treat people are available everywhere. Safe burial teams are providing safe and dignified burial services everywhere and the result is that we're seeing the beginnings of the outbreak slowing down."

At first, schools in Ebola-stricken nations of West Africa closed in response to the crisis. As they began to reopen, educational Ebola-awareness teams came to the schools to explain the basic facts of Ebola transmission and how to stay safe. Illustrated charts helped pass the message.

The WHO declared Liberia free of Ebola in early May 2015. However, six new cases appeared in July 2015 in Liberia. And scattered cases were still breaking out in Sierra Leone and Guinea. Is the epidemic in West Africa drawing to a close? What is the significance of the new cases? "We're proud of what we collectively managed to do but we need to remain vigilant," Peter Jan Graaff of the United Nations said. "The virus is not yet out of the region and as long as the virus is in the region we're still all of us potentially at risk."

An article in the *New York Times* in June 2015 suggested that Ebola may have been lying in wait in the rain forests of West Africa for many years. Until the 2014 Ebola epidemic in that region, all known outbreaks had occurred in a large swathe of Central Africa, stretching from coastal Gabon, through the Congo, and into Uganda. Scientists have found antibodies in human blood in fourteen other countries with no known Ebola cases, including Panama in Central America and the Philippines in the western Pacific. That suggests people had been exposed but had not become ill. Researchers have also identified twenty-two African countries as likely Ebola danger zones. And as humans continue to encroach on forests only inhabited by animals, it seems certain that more outbreaks will occur.

No one can be sure what will happen in the future. In the twenty-first century, we are all citizens of the world. We travel far and wide, whether by canoe between Guinea and Sierra Leone or by jet between Monrovia and London, and on to Los Angeles and New York. Borders are only lines on a map, after all, and we cannot be complacent. We cannot afford to forget how quickly Ebola and other diseases can spread and get out of control. However, Ebola taught world health officials much about how to identify and contain a dangerous infectious disease. We are better prepared for Ebola if—or when—it returns.

## DOES EBOLA HAVE A FUTURE?

Some experts believe it will be difficult or impossible to eradicate a disease that lives in animals. An article in *Global Medicine* said that to eradicate a disease, "Humans must be the only host of the agent. Animal reservoirs significantly complicate the eradication process." In the case of Ebola, as long as people are exposed to the animal reservoir—probably bats—there is a possibility of future outbreaks.

It is possible to eradicate a disease that lives only in humans. For example, smallpox was one of the most devastating diseases ever known. It had no animal reservoir. It only sickened and killed humans. Through aggressive contact tracing and vaccination programs, world health officials eradicated smallpox in 1977. Polio also is a disease that only affects people. Polio infections have fallen by 99 percent since 1988 because of the success of vaccination programs. However, polio remains endemic in Pakistan, Nigeria, and Afghanistan, largely because of social and political challenges in vaccinating children.

# GLOSSARY

**antibodies:** proteins produced in the body to help defend against foreign organisms such as viruses and bacteria

**antigens:** the proteins carried by organisms such as viruses and bacteria that trigger the immune system to send antibodies to destroy them

**Centers for Disease Control and Prevention (CDC):** a US federal agency based in Atlanta, Georgia, that is responsible for protecting the health, safety, and security of Americans through detecting and responding to emerging health threats, research, and providing data about healthy lifestyles

**clinical trials:** a series of systematic steps to study how new medications work in humans prior to legal approval of a drug for distribution and sale

**contact tracing:** identifying the people with whom an infected person has been in contact, as a measure health-care workers take to help stop the spread of diseases such as Ebola

**deoxyribonucleic nucleic acid (DNA):** the chemical material that carries genetic information for most organisms

**Doctors Without Borders:** the international aid organization that sends doctors and health-care workers to areas in need around the world. The organization is known in much of the world by its French name, Médecins Sans Frontières (MSF).

**doffing:** the process of removing personal protective equipment such as gowns, gloves, and masks in such a way as to protect the wearer from catching or spreading a disease

**donning:** the process of putting on personal protective equipment such as gowns, gloves, and masks to protect the wearer from becoming infected with a disease

**Ebola:** a dangerous virus that caused an epidemic in West Africa beginning in 2014. Possibly carried by bats, the disease is known to spread through contact with human blood, saliva, feces, vomit, and semen. It causes fever, hemorrhagic bleeding, and organ failure. The disease was first identified in Africa in 1976.

**endemic:** belonging to a region; an endemic disease, such as malaria, is constantly present within a regional population

**epidemic:** the occurrence of a disease, such as Ebola in 2014, that strikes many people in several regions at the same time

**glycoproteins:** proteins that make up the fatty membrane that surrounds the Ebola virus

**hemorrhagic fever:** a disease caused by some viruses, including Ebola, that can lead to failure of body organs, high fever, and hemorrhage (heavy bleeding)

**host:** an organism (plant or animal) infected by a pathogen such as a virus, in which the host becomes ill or dies from the infection

**incubation period:** the time between exposure to an infectious organism and the appearance of the first symptoms

**informed consent:** permission a patient grants through signing legal documents to allow a doctor to perform a treatment. The documents acknowledge the patient is aware of the possible risks and benefits of the treatment, including death.

**Marburg virus disease:** a hemorrhagic viral disease related to Ebola. Often fatal, Marburg was first identified in 1967 in three European cities.

**mutation:** a random and spontaneous change in an organism's genetic code

**pandemic:** the occurrence of a disease that affects many people in many parts of the world at the same time

**patient zero:** the first known case of a new disease outbreak. In the 2014 Ebola epidemic, patient zero was a boy called Emile in Guinea believed to have had the first case of Ebola.

**personal protective equipment (PPE):** the clothing, mask, gloves, aprons, and other gear worn to lessen exposure to a disease carried by infectious people or materials

**placebo:** a pretend or inert medicine often given to some participants in clinical trials to see if the real medicine works

**plasma:** the liquid part of blood without the red blood cells. Plasma contains antibodies, which help defend the body from disease.

**quarantine:** keeping infected or possibly infected people away from those with no exposure to an organism. The protocol may involve quarantine in a home or a medical setting.

**replicate:** to duplicate. This term is used to describe how viruses—which are not living organisms—duplicate themselves through a process that does not involve sexual reproduction.

**reservoir:** an organism (plant or animal) that carries a pathogen such as a virus without succumbing to it. The reservoir for Ebola is likely bats, although this has not yet been proven.

**ribonucleic acid (RNA):** the chemical material that carries genetic information for certain simple viruses, such as Ebola. While higher life-forms contain both DNA and RNA, viruses are unique in that they contain either DNA or RNA.

**United Nations (UN):** an international organization of 193 countries, founded in 1945. Among other tasks, the UN takes action on issues confronting humanity, such as peace, security, climate change, and human rights. It works on health emergencies through its specialized agency, the World Health Organization.

**vaccine:** a chemical substance that stimulates the immune system to produce antibodies against specific organisms such as the virus that causes measles or the bacteria that causes tetanus. Doctors typically administer vaccines through injection, although some, such as the polio and typhoid vaccines, can be given by mouth.

**virus:** a simple infective agent such as the Ebola virus that can only multiply inside the living cells of a host or reservoir

**World Health Organization (WHO):** a specialized agency of the United Nations that provides leadership on global health matters and monitors and assesses health trends

**ZMapp:** an experimental medication for Ebola that has shown promise in clinical trials for treating Ebola. The medication contains three anti-Ebola antibodies.

**zoonosis:** an infectious disease such as Ebola that is passed from animal to humans

# SOURCE NOTES

9    Peter Piot, in "Surviving Ebola," *PBS*, October 8, 2014, http://video.pbs.org/video/2365340607/.

10    Peter Piot, "Part One: A Virologist's Tale of Africa's First Encounter with Ebola," *Science*, August 11, 2014, http://news.sciencemag.org/africa/2014/08/part-one-virologists-tale-africas-first-encounter-ebola.

10    Ibid.

11    Ibid.

11    Ibid.

12    Ibid.

12    Peter Piot, in Rob Brown, "The Virus Detective Who Discovered Ebola in 1976," *BBC*, July 17, 2014, http://www.bbc.com/news/magazine-28262541.

12    Piot, "Part One: A Virologist's Tale."

12–13    Peter Piot, "Part Two: A Virologist's Tale of Africa's First Encounter with Ebola," *Science*, August 13, 2014, http://news.sciencemag.org/africa/2014/08/part-two-virologists-tale-africas-first-encounter-ebola.

14    Ibid.

15–16    Ibid.

16–17    Ibid.

17    Piot, in Brown, "The Virus Detective."

19    Piot, "Surviving Ebola."

25    Ruth Tam, "This Is How You Get Ebola as Explained by Science," *PBS NewsHour*, September 30, 2014, http://www.pbs.org/newshour/updates/know-enemy/.

28    A. Altman et al, "12 Answers to Ebola's Hard Questions," *Time*, October 23, 2014, http://time.com/3533565/12-answers-to-ebolas-hard-questions/.

29    William Schaffner, in Lara Pullen, "Public Health Specialists Warn Ebola May Still Surprise," *Medscap*, February 23, 2015, http://www.medscape.com/viewarticle/840210.

31    Margaret Chan, "UN Declares Ebola Outbreak Global International Public Health Emergency," UN News Centre, August, 8, 2014. http://www.un.org/apps/news/story.asp?NewsID=48440#.VITWeTHF_To.

35    Remy Lamah, in Ougna Camara, "Guinea Bans Bat Eating to Curb Ebola Spread, Warns on Rats," *Bloomberg Business*, March 26, 2014. http://www.bloomberg.com/news/articles/2014-03-26/guinea-bans-eating-of-bats-to-limit-ebola-spread-warns-on-rats.

36–37 Foday Gallah, in David von Drehle and Aryn Baker, "The Ones Who Answered the Call," *Time* 184, no. 24/25 (December 22, 2014): 70–107.

37 Philip Ireland, in von Drehle and Baker, "The Ones Who Answered."

40–41 Jeffrey Gold, in Maggie Fox, "Cost to Treat Ebola: $1 Million for Two Patients," *NBC News*, November 18, 2014, http://www.nbcnews.com /storyline/ebola-virus-outbreak/cost-treat-ebola-1-million-two-patients -n250986.

45 Editorial, "Ebola and Quarantine," *NEJM*, November 20, 2014. http://www .nejm.org/doi/full/10.1056/NEJMe1413139?query=featured_ebola.

46 Peter Piot, in Lawrence K. Altman, "There Before Ebola Had a Name," *New York Times*, October 6, 2014, http://www.nytimes.com/2014/10/07 /health/there-before-ebola-had-a-name.html. 3/7/15.

47 Rick Sacra, in Denise Grady, "Better Staffing Seen as Crucial to Ebola Treatment in Africa," *New York Times*, October 31, 2014, http://www .nytimes.com/2014/11/01/us/better-staffing-seen-as-crucial-to-ebola -treatment-in-africa.html?_r=0.

47 "He Survived Ebola. Now, Dr. Rick Sacra Explains Why He's Going Back to Liberia," *WBUR (Boston) On Point*, January 14, 2015, http://onpoint.wbur .org/2015/01/14/rick-sacra-ebola-doctor-survivor.

47–48 Jamal Gwathney, in Sheri Fink, "Treating Those Treating Ebola in Liberia," *New York Times*, November 5, 2014, http://www.nytimes.com/2014/11 /06/world/africa/treating-those-treating-ebola-in-liberia.html?_r=0.

49 Colin Bucks, in Lara Logan, "The Ebola Hot Zone," *60 Minutes*, aired November 9, 2014, http://www.cbsnews.com/news/the-ebola-hot-zone -liberia/.

49 Pares Momanyi, in Daniel Berehulak, "Braving Ebola," *New York Times*, October 31, 2014, http://www.nytimes.com/interactive/2014/10/31 /world/africa/photos-of-workers-and-survivors-braving-ebola-at-a-clinic-in -liberia.html?_r=3.

50 Karlyn Beer, PhD, Epidemic Intelligence Service officer, CDC. Personal interviews with the author, November 2014–February 2015.

53 Logan, "The Ebola Hot Zone."

54 David Nabarro, in Stephanie Nebehay, "Secret Burials Thwarting Efforts to Stamp Out Ebola—UN," *Reuters*, February 6, 2015, http://in.reuters .com/article/2015/02/05/health-ebola-who-idINKBN0L92Q320150205.

55 "New WHO Safe and Dignified Burial Protocol Key to Reducing Ebola Transmission," WHO, November 7, 2014. http://www.who.int/mediacentre /news/notes/2014/ebola-burial-protocol/en/.

56   "Interim Guidance for Dog or Cat Quarantine after Exposure to a Human with Confirmed Ebola Virus Disease," CDC, October 10, 2014, http://www.cdc.gov/vhf/ebola/pdf/dog-cat-quarantine.pdf.

57   "New WHO Safe and Dignified Burial Protocol Key to Reducing Ebola Transmission," WHO, November 7, 2014, http://www.who.int/mediacentre/news/notes/2014/ebola-burial-protocol/en/.

59   Barack Obama, "Letter from the President—Emergency Appropriations Request for Ebola for Fiscal Year 2015," letter to Congress, Office of the Press Secretary, November 5, 2014, http://www.whitehouse.gov/the-press-office/2014/11/05/letter-president-emergency-appropriations-request-ebola-fiscal-year-2015.

61   Gregory Hartl, in Saliou Samb, "WHO Says Guinea Ebola Outbreak Small as MSF Slams International Response," *Reuters*, April 1, 2014, http://www.reuters.com/article/2014/04/01/us-guinea-ebola-idUSBREA301X120140401.

61   Bart Janssens, in Kashmira Gander, "Ebola Outbreak: Virus Is 'Totally Out of Control' Warns Doctors Without Borders Medic," *Independent* (London), June 20, 2014, http://www.independent.co.uk/news/world/africa/ebola-outbreak-virus-is-totally-out-of-control-warns-doctors-without-borders-medic-9553337.html

62   Gregg Gonsalves and Peter Staley, "Panic, Paranoia, and Public Health—the AIDS Epidemic's Lessons for Ebola," *New England Journal of Medicine*, November 5, 2014, http://www.nejm.org/doi/full/10.1056/NEJMp1413425.

62–63  Paul Waldman, "Americans Are Terrified of Ebola. Which Could Makt It Harder to Stop Ebola," *Washington Post*, October 14, 2014, http://www.washingtonpost.com/blogs/plum-line/wp/2014/10/14/americans-are-terrified-of-ebola-which-could-make-it-harder-to-stop-ebola/.

63   Maggie Fox, "Report Slams U.S. Ebola Response and Readiness," *NBC News*, February 26, 2015, http://www.nbcnews.com/storyline/ebola-virus-outbreak/report-slams-u-s-ebola-response-readiness-n313251.

65   Isabelle Nuttall, "Ebola Travel: Vigilance, Not Bans," WHO, November 5, 2014, http://www.who.int/mediacentre/commentaries/ebola-travel/en/.

66   Peter Hotez, in Liz Szabo, "U.S. Designates 35 Hospitals as Ebola Centers," *USA Today*, December 3, 2014, http://www.usatoday.com/story/news/nation/2014/12/02/35-ebola-hospitals/19780679/.

67   Beer interview.

67–68   "Ebola Response: Where Are We Now?" MSF Briefing Paper, December 2014, http://www.doctorswithoutborders.org/sites/usa/files/ebola_briefing_paper_12.14.pdf.

69   William Fischer, in Alan Zarembo, "Ebola Suits Keep Wearers Safe If All Rules Are Followed, Experts Say," *LA Times*, October 17, 2014, http://www.latimes.com/nation/la-na-ebola-suit-20141016-html-htmlstory.html.

69   Fatu Kekula, in Elizabeth Cohen and John Bonifield, "'Fearless' Ebola Nurse Trains at Emory University," *CNN*, April 20, 2015, http://www.cnn.com/2015/04/10/health/fatu-kekula-nursing-emory/.

70   Jeremy Farrar and Peter Piot, "The Ebola Emergency—Immediate Action, Ongoing Strategy," *New England Journal of Medicine*, October 16, 2014, http://www.nejm.org/doi/full/10.1056/NEJMe1411471.

70–71   Beer interview.

71   Achille Guemou, in Betsy McKay et al, "Doctors Try Survivors' Blood to Treat Ebola," *Wall Street Journal*, December 5, 2014, http://www.wsj.com/articles/ebola-survivors-in-africa-offer-new-treatment-hope-their-blood-1417821483.

72   Andrew Brooks in "West African Communities Receiving Ebola's Orphans with Open Arms," *UN News Centre*, February 6, 2015, http://www.un.org/apps/news/story.asp?NewsID=50018#.

73   Margaret Nanyonga, in "Sierra Leone: Helping the Ebola Survivors Turn the Page," WHO, October 2014, http://www.who.int/features/2014/post-ebola-syndrome/en/.

73   Nancy Gibbs, "The Ebola Fighters: The Choice," *Time*, December 20, 2014, http://time.com/time-person-of-the-year-ebola-fighters-choice/.

75   Anthony Fauci, in "NIAID/GSK Experimental Ebola Vaccine Appears Safe, Prompts Immune Response," NIH, November 28, 2014, http://www.nih.gov/news/health/nov2014/niaid-28.htm.

76   Anthony Fauci, in Brady Dennis and Lenny Bernstein, "Two Americans Who Contracted Ebola in Africa Received an Experimental Serum," *Washington Post*, August 4, 2014, http://www.washingtonpost.com/national/health-science/2014/08/04/dbc44a48-1c07-11e4-ae54-0cfe1f974f8a_story.html.

76   Salim S. Abdool Karim, in Andrew Pollack, "Ebola Drug Could Save a Few Lives. But Whose?" *New York Times*, August 8, 2014, http://www.nytimes.com/2014/08/09/health/in-ebola-outbreak-who-should-get-experimental-drug.html.

76–77   Harriet A. Washington, "Make More Ebola Drug and Give It to Africans," *CNN*, August 6, 2014, http://www.cnn.com/2014/08/06/opinion /washington-ebola-zmapp-drug-africa/.

77   Laura Seay, "Ebola, Research Ethics, and the ZMapp Serum," *Washington Post*, August 6, 2014, http://www.washingtonpost.com/blogs /monkey-cage/wp/2014/08/06/ebola-research-ethics-and-the-zmapp -serum/.

78–79   Julie Ledgerwood, "The Lancet: Trial Confirms Ebola Vaccine Candidate Safe and Equally Immunogenic in Africa," American Association for the Advancement of Science, news release, December 22, 2014, http://www .eurekalert.org/pub_releases/2014-12/tl-tlt121914.php.

81   Unnamed leaders of National Democratic Congress in Volta region of Ghana, "Ghana Suspends Ebola Vaccine Trial after 'Guinea Pig' Backlash," *Yahoo! News*, June 11, 2015, http://news.yahoo.com/ghana -suspends-ebola-vaccine-trial-guinea-pig-backlash-135314562.html.

81   Margaret Chan, in "World on the Verge of an Effective Ebola Vaccine," WHO, July 31, 2015, http://www.who.int/mediacentre/news /releases/2015/effective-ebola-vaccine/en/.

81–82   Amber Vinson, in Byron Harris, "Ebola Victim Helps in Search of a Cure," *KHOU* (Houston), January 21, 2015, http://www.khou.com/story/news /health/2015/01/21/ebola-victim-helps-in-search-of-a-cure/22097649/.

82   Alan Magill, in Mckay et al, "Doctors Try Survivors' Blood."

84   Bertrand Draguez, in MSF, press release, "Preliminary Results of the JIKI Clinical Trial to Test the Efficacy of Favipiravir in Reducing Mortality in Individuals Infected by Ebola Virus in Guinea," February 24, 2015, http:// www.msf.org/article/preliminary-results-jiki-clinical-trial-test-efficacy -favipiravir-reducing-mortality.

86   Val Snewin, in Kate Kelland, "New 15-Minute Test for Ebola to Undergo Trials in West Africa," *Reuters*, November 28, 2014, http://www.reuters .com/article/2014/11/28/us-health-ebola-test-idUSKCN0JC13Z20141128.

88   Margaret Chan, "Ebola: UN Health Agency Urges Better Global Preparedness Against Future Outbreaks," *UN News Centre*, January, 25, 2015, http://www.un.org/apps/news/story.asp?NewsID=49902#. VMaC8v7F_To.

90   Laurie Garrett, in "The Ebola Review, Part 1," *Foreign Policy*, June 6, 2015, http://foreignpolicy.com/2015/06/06/ebola-review-world-health -organization-g-7-merkel/.

90–91   Joanne Liu, in "G7: The World Is No Better Prepared Today than a Year Ago to Respond to Ebola," *Médecins Sans Frontièrs*, June 3, 2015, http://www.msf.org/article/g7-world-no-better-prepared-today-year-ago-respond-ebola.

91   Ibid.

91   Thomas Frieden, in Michaeleen Doucleff, "Endless Ebola Epidemic? That's the 'Risk We Face Now,' CDC Says," *NPR*, December 15, 2014, http://www.npr.org/blogs/goatsandsoda/2014/12/15/370446566/endless-ebola-endemic-thats-the-risk-we-face-now-cdc-says.

91   David Nabarro, in Louis Charbonneau and Michelle Nichols, "Update 2—Ebola Outbreak in West Africa Appears to be Slowing Down—U.N.," *Reuters*, January 15, 2015, http://www.reuters.com/article/2015/01/15/health-ebola-un-idUSL1N0UU2QF20150115.

92   Peter Jan Graaff, in Doug Stanglin, "Liberia Is Free of Ebola, Says World Health Organization," *USA Today*, May 9, 2015, http://www.usatoday.com/story/news/world/2015/05/09/liberia-is-free-of-ebola-says-world-health-organization/27034655/.

93   Marjolijn Paauwe, "Elimination and Eradication of Diseases," *Global Medicine*, April 2009, http://globalmedicine.nl/issues/gm6/article2.pdf

# SELECTED BIBLIOGRAPHY

Altman Alex, Alice Park, Josh Sanburn, Alexandra Sifferlin, Bill Saporito, Mandy Oaklander, Tessa Berenson, Zeke Miller. "12 Answers to Ebola's Hard Questions." *Time*. http://time.com/3533565/12-answers-to-ebolas-hard -questions/.

Altman, Lawrence K. "There Before Ebola had a Name." *New York Times*, October 6, 2014. http://www.nytimes.com/2014/10/07/health/there-before -ebola-had-a-name.html.

Baker, Thomas Jerome. *Ebola Virus Disease: From Epidemic to Pandemic*. Seattle: CreateSpace Independent Publishing Platform, 2014.

Berehulak, Daniel. "Braving Ebola." *New York Times*, October 31, 2014. http:// www.nytimes.com/interactive/2014/10/31/world/africa/photos-of-workers -and-survivors-braving-ebola-at-a-clinic-in-liberia.html?_r=3.

Brown, Rob. "The Virus Detective Who Discovered Ebola in 1976." *BBC*, July 17, 2014. http://www.bbc.com/news/magazine 28262541.

Chertow, Daniel S., Christian Kleine, Jeffrey K. Edwards, Roberto Scaini, Ruggero Giuliani, and Armand Sprecher. "Ebola Virus Disease in West Africa: Clinical Manifestations and Management." *New England Journal of Medicine*, November 27, 2014. http://www.nejm.org/doi/full/10.1056/NEJMp1413084.

Doucleff, Michaeleen. "Endless Ebola Epidemic? That's The 'Risk We Face Now,' CDC Says." *National Public Radio*, December 15, 2014. http://www.npr.org /sections/goatsandsoda/2014/12/15/370446566/endless-ebola-endemic -thats-the-risk-we-face-now-cdc-says.

"Ebola Outbreaks." Centers for Disease Control and Prevention. Last modified June 8, 2015. http://www.cdc.gov/vhf/ebola/outbreaks/history/summaries.html.

"Ebola Travel: Vigilance, Not Bans." World Health Organization, November 5, 2014. http://www.who.int/mediacentre/commentaries/ebola-travel/en/.

Fauci, Anthony S. "NIAID/GSK Experimental Ebola Vaccine Appears Safe, Prompts Immune Response." *NIH News*, November 28, 2014. http://www.nih .gov/news/health/nov2014/niaid-28.htm.

Fauci, Anthony S., and Francis S. Collins. "NIH Ebola Update: Working toward Treatments and Vaccines." *NIH Director's Blog*, October 14, 2014. http:// directorsblog.nih.gov/2014/10/14/nih-ebola-update-working-toward -treatments-and-vaccines/.

Fink, Sheri. "Treating Those Treating Ebola in Liberia." *New York Times*, November 5, 2014. http://www.nytimes.com/2014/11/06/world/africa /treating-those-treating-ebola-in-liberia.html?_r=0.

Gibbs, Nancy. "The Ebola Fighters: The Choice." *Time*, December 10, 2014. http://time.com/time-person-of-the-year-ebola-fighters-choice/.

Logan, Lara. "The Ebola Hot Zone." CBS, *60 Minutes*, aired November 9, 2014. http://www.cbsnews.com/news/the-ebola-hot-zone-liberia/.

Mazumdar, Tulip. "Ebola Trials 'Best Chance' for Cure." *BBC News*, November 23, 2014. http://www.bbc.com/news/world-africa-30172921.

"New WHO Safe and Dignified Burial Protocol Key to Reducing Ebola Transmission." World Health Organization, November 7, 2014. http://www.who.int/mediacentre/news/notes/2014/ebola-burial-protocol/en/.

"No Early End to the Ebola Outbreak." World Health Organization, August 14, 2014. http://www.who.int/csr/disease/ebola/overview-20140814/en/.

Piot, Peter. "Part One: A Virologist's Tale of Africa's First Encounter with Ebola." *Science*, August 11, 2014. http://news.sciencemag.org/africa/2014/08/part-one-virologists-tale-africas-first-encounter-ebola.

———. "Part Two: A Virologist's Tale of Africa's First Encounter with Ebola." *Science*, August 13, 2014. http://news.sciencemag.org/africa/2014/08/part-two-virologists-tale-africas-first-encounter-ebola.

Quammen, David. *Ebola: The Natural and Human History of a Deadly Virus*. New York: W. W. Norton & Company, 2014.

"Sierra Leone: Helping the Ebola Survivors Turn the Page." World Health Organization, October 2014. http://www.who.int/features/2014/post-ebola-syndrome/en/.

"Surviving Ebola." *NOVA*. Produced and directed by Guy Smith. Aired October 8, 2014, Public Broadcasting System. http://video.pbs.org/video/2365340607/.

Tam, Ruth. "This Is How You Get Ebola, As Explained by Science." *PBS NewsHour*, September 30, 2014. http://www.pbs.org/newshour/updates/know-enemy/.

"2014 Ebola Outbreak in West Africa." Centers for Disease Control and Prevention. Last modified June 8, 2015. http://www.cdc.gov/vhf/ebola/outbreaks/2014-west-africa/index.html.

von Drehle, David, and Aryn Baker. "The Ones Who Answered the Call." *Time* 184, no. 24/25 (December 22, 2014): 70–107.

Westcott, Lucy. "For Health-Care Workers Fighting Ebola, the Biggest Battle Is Staying Healthy." *Newsweek*, November 7, 2014. http://www.newsweek.com/healthcare-workers-fighting-ebola-biggest-battle-staying-healthy-282821.

# FOR FURTHER INFORMATION

## Books

Barnard, Bryn. *Outbreak! Plagues That Changed History*. New York: Crown Books for Young Readers, 2005. This book describes how diseases have changed history. For example, the Black Death (bubonic and pneumonic plague caused by bacteria) led to the destruction of the feudal system, and yellow fever helped end the slave trade.

Friedlander, Mark P., Jr. *Outbreak: Disease Detectives at Work*. Minneapolis: Twenty-First Century Books, 2009. This book describes outbreaks, epidemics, and pandemics of past and present, including bioterrorism.

Herbst, Judith. *Germ Theory*. Minneapolis: Twenty-First Century Books, 2013. This book for YA readers discusses how doctors and researchers through the centuries discovered viruses and bacteria and how vaccines and antibiotics came to be.

Murphy, Jim. *An American Plague: The True and Terrifying Story of the Yellow Fever Epidemic of 1793*. New York: Clarion, 2003.
This Newbery Honor Book explores the great yellow fever epidemic that devastated Philadelphia, Pennsylvania, in 1793. During the epidemic, President George Washington fled the city to avoid infection. It took more than a century for scientists to discover the cause of yellow fever (a virus transmitted by mosquitoes) and learn how to prevent it.

Newman, Patricia. *Ebola: Facts and Fears*. Minneapolis: Millbrook Press, 2016.
Learn the truth behind the sensational headlines about the 2014 Ebola epidemic. Complete with excellent back material, this book answers the questions that kids have about Ebola in a simple yet compelling way.

Piot, Peter. *No Time to Lose: A Life in Pursuit of Deadly Viruses*. New York: W. W. Norton, 2012.
Dr. Piot writes of his career as a virologist, from his first discovery of Ebola in 1976, through his work with HIV, and back to Ebola again. This is a riveting biography primarily for adults and YA readers.

Quammen, David. *Spillover: Animal Infections and the Next Human Pandemic*. New York: W. W. Norton, 2012.
This well-known science writer tells the story of Ebola from its discovery in 1976 through the outbreaks prior to 2014. He covers how zoonotic diseases emerge from animals and move into humans. This is a great read for YA and adult audiences.

## Videos and Websites

"Ebola Dressing," Médecins Sans Frontières. 2014. 3:15.
  http://www.latimes.com/nation/la-na-ebola-suit-20141016-html-htmlstory.html.
  Health-care workers demonstrate how to don personal protective
  equipment.

"Ebola Emergency." Médecins Sans Frontières.
  http://www.msf.org.uk/ebola.
  This site includes numerous videos of varying lengths about the treatment
  centers built and run by Doctors Without Borders (MSF) and infographics
  that provide excellent information about the Ebola epidemic.

"Ebola Testimonies," International Conservation and Education Fund. 14:40. 2006.
  www.youtube.com/watch?v=nEpdHX_c3v8&index=56&list=UUfMErXcN2SMs
  JkGbzrHkAeA.
  A representative of the Lossi Gorilla Sanctuary in the Republic of the Congo
  speaks about how Ebola killed gorillas and chimpanzees. Other Africans tell
  how Ebola affected their families and villages. With English captions, the
  video shows the clash between science and traditional beliefs.

"Ebola Undressing," Médecins Sans Frontières. 2014. 3:47 minutes.
  http://www.latimes.com/nation/la-na-ebola-suit-20141016-html-htmlstory.html.
  Health-care workers demonstrate the time-consuming doffing of personal
  protective equipment.

"Fearless Ebola Nurse Trains at Emory University." *CNN*. 2015. 2:30.
  http://www.cnn.com/2015/04/10/health/fatu-kekula-nursing-emory/.
  Watch Fatu Kekula move from caring for her Ebola-stricken family in Liberia
  to becoming a nursing student at Emory University's Nell Hodgson Woodruff
  School of Nursing in Atlanta, Georgia.

"Improved PPE for Ebola Health-Care Workers." Johns Hopkins University Center
  for Bioengineering. 2014. 1:33.
  http://www.washingtonpost.com/news/post-nation/wp/2014/12/13/johns-
  hopkins-team-wins-u-s-award-for-improved-suit-to-fight-ebola/.
  See a demonstration of the innovative and award-winning personal
  protective equipment developed by an American university.

"Inside an Ebola Clinic in West Africa." Médecins Sans Frontières. 2014. 4:00.
  http://digg.com/video/inside-an-ebola-clinic-in-west-africa
  A physician tours an active Ebola treatment center from the inside.

"The Road to Zero: CDC's Response to the West African Ebola Epidemic, 2014–2015." Centers for Disease Control and Prevention. July 2015. 5:32. https://www.youtube.com/watch?v=DNBL-Exso9Q.
Learn more about the CDC response to the Ebola epidemic in West Africa and hear quotes from Dr. Tom Frieden and other top CDC officials.

"2014 West African Ebola Outbreak," World Health Organization. 2014. http://www.who.int/features/ebola/storymap/en/.
This informative site offers an interactive map and timeline with links to key events, stories, and further reading about Ebola.

## Organizations

### Centers for Disease Control and Prevention (CDC)
1600 Clifton Road
Atlanta, GA 30329
800-232-4636
http://www.cdc.gov/vhf/ebola/
The CDC's mission is to protect the health of Americans. Its Ebola site offers detailed information on all aspects of Ebola, including the epidemic itself and special sections for health-care workers, the public, travelers, airports, parents, and schools.

### Doctors Without Borders
78 rue de Lausanne
Case Postale 116
1211 Geneva 21, Switzerland
http://www.msf.org/
This organization, also known by its French name—Médecins Sans Frontières (MSF)—is an international, independent, medical humanitarian organization that delivers emergency medical care and assistance to people around the world. Search the site with the keyword "Ebola" for a wealth of information, including photos, videos, and graphics.

### World Health Organization (WHO)
Avenue Appia 20
1211 Geneva 27, Switzerland
http://www.who.int/csr/disease/ebola/en/
The WHO directs and coordinates health care for United Nations member countries. It provides leadership on global health matters and monitors and assesses health trends. The WHO Ebola page on the website offers stories, data, news releases, and detailed information for health-care professionals, the public, and UN member nations.

# INDEX

# PHOTO ACKNOWLEDGMENTS

The images in this book are used with the permission of: CDC/Frederick A. Murphy (ebola design backgrounds); © Karlyn D. Beer, Centers for Disease Control and Prevention, pp. 5, 6, 50; © Michael Christopher Brown/Magnum Photos, pp. 8–9; CDC/Dr. Lyle Conrad, p. 13; © Peter Piot, p. 15; © Scott Camazine/Alamy, pp. 18–19; © Daniel van Moll/laif/Redux, p. 23; © National Public Radio, p. 28; © John Moore/Getty Images, pp. 30–31, 48, 58–59, 74–75; © Tyler Hicks/Hulton Archive/Getty Images, p. 34; REUTERS/Joe Penney, p. 37; AP Photo/Nati Harnik, p. 40; © Laura Westlund/Independent Picture Service, pp. 42, 60; © Pascal Guyot/AFP/Getty Images, pp. 44–45, 46 (right), 52, 55; © Tim Brakemeier/AFP/Getty Images, p. 46 (left); Juan Guajardo/Fort Worth Star-Telegram/MCT/Newscom, p. 56; REUTERS/Jim Bourg, p. 63; © Seylluo/AFP/Getty Images, p. 71; © Daniel Berehulak/The New York Time/Redux, p. 72 (left); © Marcus DiPaola/NurPhoto/CORBIS, p. 72 (right); REUTERS/Steve Parsons/Pool/Newscom, p. 80; © Howard Lipin/U-T San Diego/ZUMA Wire/Alamy, p. 83; AP Photo/Choe Jae-koo, p. 87; © TANYA BINDRA/epa/CORBIS, p. 89; © SIA KAMBOU/AFP/Getty Images, p. 92.

Front cover: Marcus DiPaola/NurPhoto/Rex/Rex USA.

Jacket flaps and back cover: CDC/ Frederick A. Murphy.

## ABOUT THE AUTHOR

Connie Goldsmith has written sixteen nonfiction books for middle-school and young adult readers, mostly on health topics, and has also published more than two hundred magazine articles for adults and children. Her YA book *Bombs over Bikini* was a Junior Library Guild Selection, a Children's Book Committee at Bank Street College Best Children's Book of the Year, an Association of Children's Librarians of Northern California Distinguished Book, and an SCBWI Crystal Kite winner. She is an active member of the Society of Children's Book Writers and Illustrators and a member of the Authors Guild. Goldsmith is also a registered nurse with a bachelor of science degree in nursing and a master of public administration degree in health care. Additionally, Goldsmith writes for nurses and writes a child health column for a regional parenting magazine in Sacramento, California, where she lives.